Nature-Positive Circular Bioeconomy: Sustainable Biomass, Biobased Products, Organic Waste Recycling, and Regenerative Land Use for Climate, Biodiversity, and Resource Efficiency

I0119555

Copyright

Nature-Positive Circular Bioeconomy: Sustainable Biomass, Biobased Products, Organic Waste Recycling, and Regenerative Land Use for Climate, Biodiversity, and Resource Efficiency

© 2025 Robert C. Brears

All rights reserved.

No part of this publication may be reproduced, stored in a retrieval system, or transmitted in any form or by any means—electronic, mechanical, photocopying, recording, or otherwise—without the prior written permission of the publisher, except in the case of brief quotations used in reviews, articles, or academic analysis.

The author and publisher are of the same opinion regarding the views and content expressed in this work.

Disclaimer: The information in this book is provided for general knowledge and educational purposes only. While every effort has been made to ensure accuracy, the author and publisher make no representations or warranties with respect to the completeness or suitability of the content. The author and publisher accept no liability for any errors, omissions, or outcomes resulting from the application of information contained herein. Readers are advised to consult appropriate professionals or authorities before acting on any material presented.

ISBN (eBook): 978-1-991369-65-9

ISBN (Paperback): 978-1-991369-66-6

Published by Global Climate Solutions

First Edition, 2025

Cover design and interior layout by Global Climate Solutions

Table of Contents

Introduction

The circular bioeconomy represents a transformative approach to addressing interconnected challenges related to resource scarcity, biodiversity loss, climate change, and waste. It combines the principles of circular economy—focused on keeping materials in use and designing out waste—with the use of renewable biological resources that can regenerate naturally. In doing so, it offers a pathway to decouple economic development from environmental degradation while contributing to ecosystem restoration and climate resilience.

Unlike traditional bioeconomy models that may rely heavily on virgin biomass, a circular bioeconomy emphasizes systems that reuse, recycle, and valorize biological materials within ecological limits. It promotes the use of bio-based products, regenerative agriculture, nutrient recovery, and sustainable land use while supporting innovation in areas such as biotechnology, biomanufacturing, and digital traceability.

As momentum builds globally for sustainable economic transformation, the circular bioeconomy offers an integrated framework that links environmental goals with social and economic benefits. This publication explores the strategies, tools, and governance approaches needed to operationalize a nature-positive circular bioeconomy—one that not only reduces harm but actively restores ecosystems and supports inclusive prosperity.

Chapter 1. Conceptual Foundations of a Nature-Positive Circular Bioeconomy

The concept of a nature-positive circular bioeconomy brings together three transformative agendas: the bioeconomy, which emphasizes the use of renewable biological resources; the circular economy, which focuses on maintaining materials in use and eliminating waste; and nature-positivity, which prioritizes ecosystem restoration and biodiversity enhancement. At their intersection lies a holistic framework that aims not only to decarbonize and dematerialize economies but to regenerate natural systems while ensuring social equity.

This chapter introduces the foundational concepts, definitions, and guiding principles of a nature-positive circular bioeconomy. It explores how circularity and regeneration differ from conventional sustainability approaches by moving beyond efficiency toward systems that restore ecological function. The chapter also clarifies key terms such as bio-based systems, closed-loop cycles, ecosystem services, and natural capital, establishing a shared vocabulary for the discussion that follows.

By outlining the theoretical underpinnings and normative goals of this model, the chapter sets the stage for deeper exploration into policy, governance, technology, and finance. It provides the conceptual basis for understanding how the circular bioeconomy can align with planetary boundaries and biodiversity targets, while addressing global challenges such as climate change, land degradation, and unsustainable resource use.

Definition of Core Terms and Paradigms

A nature-positive circular bioeconomy combines elements from three interrelated concepts—bioeconomy, circular economy, and nature-positivity—each with distinct but complementary objectives. The bioeconomy refers to the production, use, and conservation of biological resources—such as crops, forests, animals, and microorganisms—to provide food, materials, chemicals, and energy in a sustainable manner. It focuses on reducing reliance on fossil fuels and enhancing the role of renewable biological inputs in economic systems.

The circular economy is an economic model designed to eliminate waste, keep products and materials in use for as long as possible, and regenerate natural systems. It contrasts with the linear model of "take-make-dispose" by emphasizing restorative and regenerative design. In a circular economy, materials are continuously cycled through the economy, with minimal input of virgin resources and reduced environmental pressures.

Nature-positivity introduces an ecological lens that seeks to halt and reverse biodiversity loss, ensuring that human activities actively contribute to the recovery and resilience of ecosystems. This approach goes beyond "doing less harm" and aims to generate net positive outcomes for nature.

Integrating these paradigms, a nature-positive circular bioeconomy promotes the sustainable use of biological resources while maintaining or enhancing ecosystem integrity. It emphasizes systems thinking, recognizing the interconnectedness of economic, social, and ecological processes. By aligning economic development with the principles of circularity and ecological regeneration, this integrated model supports long-term sustainability, climate resilience, and biodiversity conservation.

Historical Evolution to Regenerative Models

The evolution from linear to circular and then to regenerative models reflects a growing awareness of environmental limits and the need for systemic change in how resources are produced, consumed, and managed. The linear economy, which has dominated industrial development for over a century, is based on a one-way flow of materials: extraction, production, consumption, and disposal. While effective at driving short-term economic growth, this model has led to significant environmental degradation, resource depletion, and waste accumulation.

In response, the circular economy emerged as a framework aimed at reducing the environmental footprint of production and consumption. It introduced the concepts of closing resource loops, promoting product longevity, and designing out waste. Circularity brought greater efficiency to resource use and encouraged innovation in materials and business models. However, it primarily focused on economic and material flows, with limited attention to the ecological impacts of these flows on biodiversity and ecosystem services.

The regenerative model builds on and expands the circular economy by explicitly prioritizing ecological health and the restoration of natural systems. Rather than merely minimizing harm, regenerative approaches seek to restore and enhance ecosystems, soil health, water cycles, and biodiversity. This model integrates social equity, ecological function, and long-term resilience into economic systems. It is increasingly being recognized as essential for aligning economic activity with planetary boundaries and ensuring that growth is not achieved at the expense of nature.

Principles: Decoupling, Cascading Use, Regeneration, Biodiversity Value

A nature-positive circular bioeconomy is guided by a set of interrelated principles that collectively aim to reshape economic activity in line with ecological limits and social well-being. One key principle is decoupling, which refers to separating economic growth from environmental degradation. This can be relative—where impacts grow more slowly than the economy—or absolute—where impacts decline while the economy continues to grow. In the context of bio-based systems, decoupling involves reducing land, water, and energy use per unit of output and minimizing negative impacts on biodiversity and ecosystem services.

8

Another central concept is cascading use, which promotes the sequential utilization of biomass to extract the highest possible value from it before final disposal or energy recovery. For example, a single biomass input might first be used for material applications, then converted to animal feed, and ultimately utilized for energy generation. Cascading prioritizes applications with the greatest economic and environmental returns, extending the functional lifespan of bio-based resources.

Regeneration goes beyond reuse and recycling by focusing on restoring natural capital. This includes practices that enhance soil fertility, re-establish native vegetation, rehabilitate degraded landscapes, and support ecological processes that sustain life. Regenerative approaches are designed to create positive feedback loops where natural systems are strengthened over time.

The principle of biodiversity value ensures that economic processes recognize, respect, and enhance the variety of life on Earth. Rather than treating biodiversity as a constraint, this principle integrates it as a foundational asset—essential for ecosystem function, resilience, and productivity. In a nature-positive circular bioeconomy, biodiversity is not just protected but actively supported through land-use choices, supply chain practices, and product design that create or restore habitats, maintain species diversity, and preserve ecosystem functions.

Nature-Positive vs Circular Bioeconomy

While the circular bioeconomy and the nature-positive circular bioeconomy share common goals—such as reducing waste, optimizing resource use, and fostering sustainable economic activity—they differ in scope, emphasis, and environmental ambition. A circular bioeconomy primarily focuses on substituting fossil-based materials with renewable biological resources, closing material loops, and increasing the efficiency of biomass utilization. It emphasizes economic innovation and sustainability through improved resource management, often with a focus on product design, bio-based technologies, and market development.

However, circular bioeconomy models do not always account for the ecological consequences of increased biomass demand or land-use changes. For instance, without safeguards, scaling up bio-based production could contribute to deforestation, habitat loss, and monoculture expansion. In this sense, circularity alone does not guarantee positive outcomes for biodiversity or ecosystem health.

In contrast, a nature-positive circular bioeconomy integrates biodiversity and ecosystem regeneration into the core of its design. It explicitly aims to reverse nature loss by embedding ecological considerations in every stage of the bio-based value chain. This model prioritizes nature as a beneficiary of economic activity, not merely a resource input. It encourages the restoration of ecosystems, supports multifunctional landscapes, and promotes practices that increase ecological resilience.

Crucially, the nature-positive approach includes safeguards against overexploitation and promotes land-use strategies that balance biomass production with habitat preservation. It reflects a shift from sustainable use to regenerative outcomes, where the success of economic systems is measured not just by reduced harm but by positive contributions to nature. This makes it a more holistic and ambitious model, suitable for addressing the interlinked challenges of biodiversity loss, climate change, and unsustainable resource use.

Systems Thinking and Lifecycle Perspective

A nature-positive circular bioeconomy relies on systems thinking to understand and manage the complex interdependencies between economic activities, ecological processes, and social outcomes. Systems thinking moves beyond isolated interventions and considers entire value chains, feedback loops, and cross-sectoral interactions. It recognizes that actions taken in one part of a system—such as intensifying biomass production—can have unintended consequences elsewhere, such as land degradation or biodiversity loss. By adopting this holistic perspective, decision-makers can identify synergies, trade-offs, and leverage points for systemic transformation.

One of the key tools within systems thinking is the lifecycle perspective, which assesses the environmental and social impacts of a product or process from cradle to grave—or ideally, cradle to cradle in circular systems. This includes resource extraction, production, distribution, use, reuse, and end-of-life management. Lifecycle thinking enables a comprehensive understanding of where impacts occur, where value can be retained, and where interventions are most effective.

In a nature-positive context, lifecycle assessments must extend beyond carbon footprints or material efficiency to also include biodiversity impacts, ecosystem service flows, and regenerative potential. For example, a bio-based product may have low emissions but could still contribute to habitat conversion or invasive species introduction if not carefully sourced and managed. Therefore, evaluating impacts holistically ensures that circular solutions do not shift burdens elsewhere in the system.

Incorporating systems and lifecycle thinking also supports better governance, as it provides evidence for integrated policy-making and cross-sector coordination. It enables actors across agriculture, forestry, industry, and environmental management to align strategies in ways that promote circularity while enhancing ecosystem health. Ultimately, these approaches underpin the design of economic systems that function within planetary boundaries and contribute positively to nature.

Global Policy Alignment and Frameworks

Achieving a nature-positive circular bioeconomy requires alignment with international policy frameworks that promote sustainability, biodiversity conservation, and climate resilience. These global frameworks provide guiding principles, measurable targets, and mechanisms for cooperation across borders, sectors, and governance levels.

One of the most relevant frameworks is the 2030 Agenda for Sustainable Development, particularly Sustainable Development Goals (SDGs) such as SDG 12 (Responsible Consumption and Production), SDG 13 (Climate Action), SDG 14 (Life Below Water), and SDG 15 (Life on Land). A nature-positive circular bioeconomy directly contributes to these goals by promoting regenerative resource use, reducing pollution, and enhancing ecosystem services.

The Kunming-Montreal Global Biodiversity Framework (GBF) adopted under the Convention on Biological Diversity (CBD) sets ambitious goals for halting and reversing biodiversity loss by 2030. It emphasizes integrating biodiversity into all sectors of the economy, including agriculture, forestry, and infrastructure. A circular bioeconomy aligned with GBF principles must ensure that economic activities contribute to ecosystem restoration, avoid conversion of natural habitats, and reduce pressures on species and genetic diversity.

In parallel, the Paris Agreement on Climate Change encourages low-emission development pathways and nature-based solutions to meet national climate targets (NDCs). The bioeconomy can contribute by reducing reliance on fossil fuels and increasing carbon sequestration through practices like regenerative agriculture and sustainable forestry. However, safeguards are needed to avoid trade-offs, such as land-use changes that undermine climate or biodiversity goals.

Other relevant frameworks include the UN Decade on Ecosystem Restoration, the EU Circular Economy Action Plan, and the OECD's Bioeconomy to 2030 strategy, all of which stress the integration of ecological regeneration into economic planning. Aligning national bioeconomy strategies with these global instruments enables coherence, improves access to international financing and partnerships, and supports consistent metrics for monitoring progress.

Ultimately, policy alignment ensures that the shift to a nature-positive circular bioeconomy is not pursued in isolation but is embedded in a wider system of global commitments aimed at ensuring a just and sustainable future for people and the planet.

Chapter 2. Biomass Resource Governance and Regeneration

Biomass lies at the core of the circular bioeconomy, serving as the renewable feedstock for bio-based products, energy, and materials. However, the sustainability of biomass use depends on how resources are governed, managed, and regenerated across landscapes and supply chains. Without proper oversight, biomass extraction can contribute to deforestation, biodiversity loss, soil degradation, and competition for land.

This chapter introduces the governance frameworks and regenerative practices necessary to ensure that biomass sourcing supports long-term ecological health and contributes to nature-positive outcomes. It examines the types of biomass relevant to the circular bioeconomy—such as agricultural residues, forestry by-products, marine resources, and organic waste—and the principles guiding their sustainable production and use.

The chapter also explores how policies, certification schemes, and land-use planning tools can align biomass utilization with ecosystem protection, equitable access, and climate goals. Special attention is given to the importance of managing trade-offs between competing land uses (e.g. food, feed, fuel, fiber, and habitat) and the role of agroecological systems and community stewardship in supporting regeneration.

By framing biomass as both a material input and a living system, this chapter underscores the need for governance approaches that balance resource productivity with the protection and restoration of ecological integrity.

Types of Biomass: Forestry, Agriculture, Marine, Organic Waste

Biomass, the biological material used as feedstock in a circular bioeconomy, can be categorized into four primary types: forestry biomass, agricultural biomass, marine biomass, and organic waste. Each type presents unique opportunities and challenges in advancing a nature-positive circular bioeconomy and requires careful management to align with ecological sustainability and biodiversity goals.

Forestry biomass includes roundwood, residues such as branches, bark, sawdust, and wood chips derived from logging and wood processing. It can be used in construction, paper production, bioenergy, and as input for bio-based materials. To ensure environmental integrity, forestry biomass must be sourced from sustainably managed forests that preserve ecosystem services, protect native biodiversity, and prevent land degradation.

Agricultural biomass consists of food and non-food crops, crop residues (e.g., husks, straw), livestock manure, and processing by-products. This biomass supports a wide range of applications, including biofuels, bioplastics, animal feed, and fertilizers. Sustainable use requires maintaining soil health, reducing chemical inputs, optimizing water use, and avoiding expansion into ecologically sensitive areas.

Marine biomass encompasses seaweed, algae, and residues from fish processing. These resources offer high productivity with limited land requirements and are suitable for biochemicals, bio-packaging, food, and feed. However, marine biomass development must address risks such as nutrient imbalance, habitat disruption, and conflicts with local fisheries or conservation areas.

Organic waste includes food waste, green waste, sewage sludge, and industrial bio-waste. This category plays a vital role in the circular economy by enabling nutrient recovery, composting, anaerobic digestion, and bioenergy generation. Valorizing organic waste reduces landfill dependency and prevents methane emissions, but contamination and collection efficiency remain challenges.

Understanding these biomass types supports targeted policy and technology development. In a nature-positive framework, biomass must be mobilized without compromising ecosystem stability, ensuring that circular solutions reinforce ecological resilience rather than shifting environmental burdens elsewhere.

Principles for Sustainable Biomass Production and Harvesting

Sustainable biomass production and harvesting form the foundation of a nature-positive circular bioeconomy. These principles ensure that the use of biological resources does not lead to ecosystem degradation, biodiversity loss, or social inequity. Instead, they promote regenerative practices that maintain or enhance the natural capital on which bio-based systems depend.

The first principle is resource renewability, which requires that biomass is harvested at a rate that does not exceed the ecosystem's capacity to regenerate. This applies across agricultural, forestry, and marine systems. Harvesting must respect ecological thresholds, such as maintaining soil organic matter, preserving tree canopy cover, or ensuring the reproductive cycles of marine species.

Second is the protection of biodiversity and ecosystem functions. Biomass production must avoid converting high-value conservation areas, wetlands, or intact forests into cultivation zones. Habitat fragmentation, monoculture expansion, and chemical-intensive farming can undermine species richness and disrupt ecological processes. Integrating buffer zones, maintaining habitat corridors, and applying mixed cropping or polyculture techniques help support biodiversity.

A third principle is soil and water stewardship. Biomass production should enhance soil fertility, prevent erosion, and maintain water quality and availability. Practices such as cover cropping, reduced tillage, organic amendments, and efficient irrigation support these goals. In forestry, maintaining root structures, minimizing clear-cutting, and managing riparian zones contribute to ecosystem health.

Climate resilience and emissions reduction are also critical. Biomass systems should contribute to climate mitigation by enhancing carbon sequestration in soils and vegetation while minimizing emissions from fertilizer use, land-use change, and transport. Sustainable forestry and agroforestry, for instance, can serve as carbon sinks if well-managed.

Social and land tenure considerations must not be overlooked. Sustainable biomass production respects the rights of local communities, avoids land grabbing, and supports equitable benefit-sharing. Participatory governance and community-based management approaches are essential to align economic development with social justice.

Finally, monitoring and certification ensure transparency and accountability. Voluntary certification schemes (e.g., FSC, RSPO, organic labels) and national sustainability standards can help verify compliance with environmental and social criteria. However, these systems must be robust, context-sensitive, and accessible to small producers.

Adhering to these principles helps ensure that biomass feedstocks are not only renewable but regenerative—supporting a bioeconomy that builds, rather than depletes, ecological and social capital.

Avoiding Overexploitation and Land-Use Conflicts

A critical challenge in scaling the circular bioeconomy lies in ensuring that increased demand for biomass does not lead to overexploitation of natural resources or intensify land-use conflicts. Without effective safeguards, the expansion of bio-based industries risks undermining the very ecological foundations they aim to support. Addressing these risks requires integrated land-use planning, clear sustainability thresholds, and policies that balance multiple objectives—economic, environmental, and social.

Overexploitation occurs when biological resources are extracted at a rate that exceeds the regenerative capacity of ecosystems. This is particularly relevant for forestry, marine biomass, and non-timber forest products, where short-term economic pressures may incentivize unsustainable harvesting. Overharvesting can degrade soil fertility, reduce biodiversity, disrupt carbon and nutrient cycles, and compromise water systems. To prevent this, biomass extraction must be grounded in ecosystem-based management approaches that set ecological limits, informed by scientific monitoring and adaptive feedback.

Land-use conflicts arise when competing demands for land—such as food production, bioenergy, conservation, and urban development—intersect. The expansion of biomass production for industrial or energy purposes can displace food crops, reduce land availability for nature conservation, or impact the rights of indigenous and local communities. A nature-positive circular bioeconomy must avoid replicating the issues associated with large-scale monocultures and land conversion for first-generation biofuels.

Key strategies to mitigate land-use conflicts include:

- Prioritizing marginal, degraded, or underutilized lands for biomass production, where ecological restoration and productive use can go hand in hand
- Encouraging multi-functional landscapes, such as agroforestry or integrated farming systems, that combine biomass production with biodiversity and ecosystem service benefits
- Improving biomass yields sustainably through ecological intensification and better management practices, reducing the need for land expansion
- Valorizing organic waste and secondary biomass streams, which minimizes pressure on primary production systems

- Implementing spatial planning tools and stakeholder engagement, particularly at the landscape or watershed level, to balance competing needs and ensure inclusive governance

Ultimately, avoiding overexploitation and land-use conflict is not just about limiting harm but about designing biomass systems that are resilient, equitable, and capable of contributing to ecological restoration. This aligns with the broader goals of a nature-positive transition, where land is managed not only for productivity but for long-term ecosystem integrity and social well-being.

Promoting Agroecological Systems, Regenerative Agriculture, and Sustainable Forestry

Transitioning to a nature-positive circular bioeconomy requires a shift from input-intensive production systems to approaches that work with, rather than against, ecological processes. Three key land-use strategies—agroecological systems, regenerative agriculture, and sustainable forestry—offer frameworks to produce biomass in ways that restore soil health, enhance biodiversity, and strengthen ecosystem services, while supporting long-term productivity and resilience.

Agroecological systems integrate ecological principles into farming practices, emphasizing diversity, resilience, and resource efficiency. These systems rely on biological inputs and interactions—such as nitrogen fixation, pest control through biodiversity, and nutrient cycling—to reduce dependency on synthetic chemicals and fossil fuels. Agroecology also promotes polycultures, intercropping, agroforestry, and crop-livestock integration to mimic natural ecosystems. In doing so, it contributes to higher functional biodiversity, improved soil structure, and better water retention, aligning production with conservation goals.

Regenerative agriculture takes these principles further by aiming to actively restore degraded land and improve ecosystem functioning. Core practices include minimal soil disturbance (e.g., no-till or reduced-till farming), permanent soil cover, crop rotation, composting, and managed grazing. These methods enhance soil organic matter, increase carbon sequestration, improve water infiltration, and strengthen the land's capacity to recover from stressors such as drought or disease. Regenerative agriculture prioritizes outcomes—such as enhanced ecosystem health—rather than specific inputs, making it flexible across different landscapes and cultures.

Sustainable forestry balances the productive use of forest resources with the preservation of ecological integrity. It involves careful planning of harvest cycles, protection of high conservation value forests, retention of structural diversity (e.g., deadwood, canopy layers), and maintenance of natural regeneration processes. Certification schemes and national forest policies often guide sustainable practices, but on-the-ground implementation depends on strong governance, monitoring, and local participation. Sustainable forestry also supports the bioeconomy by providing renewable materials—such as timber, fibers, and lignocellulosic biomass—while sequestering carbon and preserving habitats.

Together, these approaches provide a foundation for biomass production that is not only sustainable but regenerative. They prioritize soil health, biodiversity, water conservation, and climate mitigation as integral components of productivity. In a circular bioeconomy, such practices ensure that the sourcing of biological resources contributes to environmental restoration, rather than depletion. Embedding agroecological and regenerative principles across biomass systems is therefore essential to achieve a truly nature-positive transformation.

Governance Tools for Ecosystem Protection and Restoration in Biomass Supply Chains

Effective governance is critical to ensuring that biomass supply chains support, rather than undermine, ecosystem protection and restoration. Governance tools help establish clear rules, enforce compliance, incentivize positive practices, and align stakeholder actions across the biomass value chain. In the context of a nature-positive circular bioeconomy, these tools must promote ecological integrity, transparency, and long-term sustainability from resource extraction through to end use.

One key governance tool is the environmental licensing and permitting system, which regulates land-use changes, harvesting limits, and pollution controls. By requiring environmental impact assessments (EIAs) and restoration plans as prerequisites for biomass-related activities, authorities can prevent ecosystem degradation and monitor compliance. Licensing frameworks can be enhanced by integrating biodiversity safeguards and ecosystem service valuations into approval criteria.

Zoning and spatial planning instruments—such as land-use classifications, conservation set-asides, and ecological corridors— can direct biomass production away from high-biodiversity or ecologically sensitive areas. Landscape-level planning approaches support multifunctional land use, enabling both economic activity and conservation goals to coexist. These tools can also be used to identify priority areas for ecological restoration, aligning supply chain expansion with nature recovery targets.

Sustainability standards and certification schemes (e.g., Forest Stewardship Council, Roundtable on Sustainable Biomaterials) are widely used voluntary governance tools that promote responsible sourcing practices. These schemes often include criteria for biodiversity protection, water stewardship, soil conservation, and community rights. While voluntary, they influence market behavior and enable buyers to select biomass that meets defined environmental and social performance benchmarks.

Monitoring and traceability systems, supported by digital technologies such as blockchain and geospatial platforms, enhance transparency across supply chains. They allow regulators, companies, and consumers to verify the origin of biomass, assess land-use impacts, and track compliance with sustainability requirements. These systems are essential for enforcing rules and detecting violations such as illegal logging or unsanctioned land clearing.

Economic instruments and incentives also play a role in governance. Payments for ecosystem services (PES), biodiversity offset schemes, and tax benefits for sustainable practices can shift the economic calculus in favor of ecosystem-friendly biomass production. At the same time, penalties for non-compliance and the removal of harmful subsidies (e.g., for chemical fertilizers or land conversion) are necessary to discourage damaging practices.

Stakeholder engagement and participatory governance ensure that decisions reflect local needs and ecological realities. Involving landowners, indigenous groups, and community organizations in the design and oversight of biomass governance enhances legitimacy and improves environmental outcomes.

Collectively, these governance tools help create the enabling environment for biomass supply chains that are both circular and nature-positive. They support integrated, cross-sectoral decision-making, uphold environmental and social standards, and embed restoration into economic activity.

Managing Trade-Offs Between Food, Feed, Fuel, Fiber, and Nature

The expansion of the circular bioeconomy intensifies competition for land and biomass among multiple end-uses: food, animal feed, bioenergy and fuels, fiber and materials, and the conservation of nature. Managing these trade-offs is essential to ensure that resource use supports social needs and ecological integrity without displacing critical functions or exacerbating environmental pressures. A nature-positive circular bioeconomy must prioritize multifunctionality and systemic efficiency over maximization of any single output.

The food versus fuel debate is one of the most visible trade-offs, particularly where energy crops displace land previously used for food production or ecosystems. While bioenergy can contribute to decarbonization, large-scale cultivation of first-generation biofuel crops—such as maize or palm oil—can threaten food security, drive deforestation, and increase emissions through land-use change. To address this, policies should favor residues and waste-based feedstocks for bioenergy and support decentralized energy solutions that complement rather than compete with food systems.

Animal feed represents another major demand on agricultural land, especially in high-input livestock systems. Converting land to grow feed instead of human food reduces caloric efficiency and increases environmental impact. A circular bioeconomy can ease this pressure by encouraging alternative protein sources, such as algae, insects, or fermentation-derived feeds, and by redirecting food waste and crop residues toward feed, where safe and feasible.

Fiber and industrial materials derived from biomass—including bioplastics, textiles, and packaging—offer renewable alternatives to fossil-based products. However, scaling up these sectors without sustainability controls could divert land from food and nature, particularly in markets driven by rising demand and short innovation cycles. Implementing material hierarchy principles, such as prioritizing long-lived applications and encouraging reuse, helps reduce the intensity of land competition.

Conservation of nature and ecosystem services must be treated as a non-negotiable pillar. Preserving biodiversity, carbon sinks, water regulation, and pollination cannot be subordinate to short-term economic gains. Tools such as land-use zoning, ecological compensation, and mandatory conservation set-asides can help secure nature's share. Moreover, applying true-cost accounting methods—including environmental and social externalities—enables more balanced evaluation of biomass uses.

To manage these trade-offs effectively, governance systems must promote integrated land-use planning, cross-sector coordination, and scenario-based impact assessments. Policies should be aligned across agriculture, energy, industry, and environment ministries, with clear sustainability thresholds to prevent crossing planetary boundaries.

Ultimately, trade-off management is not about eliminating competition, but about orchestrating synergies and minimizing conflict. A nature-positive circular bioeconomy recognizes that land is finite, ecosystems are fragile, and decisions must be made with a view to long-term resilience, equity, and ecological balance.

Chapter 3. Designing Circular and Regenerative Bio-Based Systems

The design of bio-based systems plays a critical role in determining whether they contribute to circularity and ecological regeneration or perpetuate linear, extractive patterns. A nature-positive circular bioeconomy requires products, materials, and systems that not only minimize waste and emissions but are intentionally created to return value to ecosystems through safe biodegradation, nutrient cycling, and extended material use.

This chapter explores the core principles and practical strategies for designing bio-based systems that are both circular and regenerative. It examines how ecodesign, modularity, biodegradability, and recyclability can be integrated into product development, alongside the use of bio-based materials that support closed-loop recovery and safe return to nature.

The chapter also discusses innovation in material science, including the development of bio-based alternatives to fossil-derived inputs and the role of product-service systems in extending use cycles. Attention is given to enabling technologies, such as digital product passports and biorefineries, that facilitate material tracking, modular reuse, and cascading value creation.

By focusing on upstream design decisions, this chapter highlights how product development can align with planetary boundaries and circular bioeconomy objectives, ensuring that bio-based innovation supports not only decarbonization and dematerialization but also ecological restoration and long-term resilience.

Ecodesign Principles for Bio-Based Products and Materials

Ecodesign—designing products with environmental considerations integrated from the outset—is central to ensuring that bio-based products contribute to a nature-positive circular bioeconomy. While bio-based materials offer potential sustainability advantages over fossil-based alternatives, their benefits are not guaranteed unless they are designed to be circular, low-impact, and regenerative throughout their lifecycle. Ecodesign principles help align product development with resource efficiency, durability, reuse, and ecosystem health.

The first principle is design for material efficiency, which emphasizes minimizing resource inputs and waste generation from raw material extraction through to end-of-life. For bio-based products, this includes selecting low-impact feedstocks (e.g., agricultural residues, waste biomass) and optimizing material use in manufacturing. Lightweighting, modularity, and component standardization are techniques used to reduce environmental burdens during production and use.

Design for durability and longevity ensures that products remain functional over extended periods, reducing the need for frequent replacement and additional biomass extraction. In contrast to the disposable model, ecodesign supports repairable, upgradable, and multifunctional products that retain value across multiple use cycles. This is particularly important for wood-based products, textiles, and bio-composites used in construction and consumer goods.

Design for reuse and remanufacture enables components or entire products to be easily disassembled and reintegrated into new manufacturing processes. For example, bio-based packaging systems can be designed with reusable elements or refilling mechanisms. This requires materials that can withstand multiple use cycles without degradation and interfaces that allow for easy separation and reintegration.

Design for biodegradability and compostability is especially relevant for short-lived or dispersive products such as food packaging, films, and agricultural mulch. These products should break down safely in natural or industrial composting environments without leaving harmful residues. It is essential to distinguish between genuine biodegradability and marketing claims; compostable products must meet recognized standards (e.g., EN 13432, ASTM D6400) and be suited to local waste infrastructure.

Design for closed-loop recycling focuses on material recovery pathways that retain the quality of bio-based inputs for high-value reuse. Unlike downcycling, where materials lose function over time, closed-loop systems preserve feedstock integrity through effective sorting, low-contamination material streams, and compatible chemical or mechanical recycling processes.

Another key ecodesign principle is toxicity avoidance, which ensures that bio-based materials do not introduce harmful substances into ecosystems or human health pathways. Additives, coatings, and processing agents should be carefully assessed and selected to avoid persistent pollutants or endocrine-disrupting compounds, even if the base material is renewable.

Finally, life cycle thinking must guide the application of ecodesign principles. A product's sustainability is not solely determined by its materials, but by its entire journey—from feedstock cultivation and processing to use, reuse, and eventual disposal or regeneration. By applying ecodesign holistically, bio-based products can be optimized for performance, circularity, and alignment with ecological regeneration goals.

Modular, Recyclable, and Biodegradable Product Innovation

Innovating bio-based products to be modular, recyclable, and biodegradable is essential to advancing a circular bioeconomy that is both resource-efficient and nature-positive. These three attributes—when built into the design and development phase—extend product lifespans, enable material recovery, and support safe reintegration into natural systems. They are not mutually exclusive but should be applied strategically depending on the product's function, lifespan, and end-of-life pathway.

Modular design refers to creating products composed of discrete, standardized components that can be easily separated, repaired, upgraded, or replaced. In the context of bio-based materials, modularity enables parts of a product to be reused without the need for complete disassembly or reprocessing. This is particularly relevant in furniture, packaging systems, and construction materials made from wood, mycelium composites, or bio-based polymers. Modular innovation supports resource efficiency by minimizing waste and reducing the frequency of full product replacement.

Recyclability ensures that a product or its components can be reprocessed into new materials of similar quality. For bio-based products, mechanical recycling may apply to items such as bio-based plastics or natural fiber composites, while chemical recycling can be used for more complex or contaminated materials. To be truly recyclable, products must avoid material mixing (e.g., layered materials with incompatible polymers) and be designed for easy sorting and separation. Labels, adhesives, and coatings must also be considered, as they can hinder recycling processes if not carefully selected.

Biodegradability is an essential attribute for bio-based products that are likely to be used in open environments or where retrieval is impractical—such as agricultural mulch films, fishing gear, or certain packaging types. These products should be designed to decompose through microbial action into non-toxic residues such as water, carbon dioxide, and biomass, without releasing persistent or harmful substances. It is crucial that biodegradability claims are substantiated by standards and that products are suited to local conditions—whether home composting, industrial composting, or natural soil and marine environments.

Innovative product development increasingly combines these characteristics. For instance, modular packaging systems may use recyclable rigid bio-based plastics combined with biodegradable film inserts. In construction, panels made from compressed agricultural waste can be both modular and compostable after use. Such innovations require a cross-disciplinary approach, involving materials science, engineering, design, and life cycle analysis to ensure performance is balanced with environmental integrity.

Critically, these innovations must align with real-world waste management systems. Biodegradable products that end up in landfills or incinerators offer little advantage, while recyclable products with no available recycling stream may become contaminants. Therefore, innovation must be guided by systems compatibility, ensuring that materials and designs match the available infrastructure and contribute meaningfully to circularity and regeneration goals.

Bio-Based Alternatives to Fossil-Derived Materials and Chemicals

A core component of the nature-positive circular bioeconomy is the development and scaling of bio-based alternatives to fossil-derived materials and chemicals. These substitutes aim to reduce greenhouse gas emissions, toxic pollution, and dependency on non-renewable resources, while supporting renewable feedstock use that is regenerative and biodiversity-friendly. For these alternatives to be effective, they must match or exceed the functional performance of fossil-based counterparts and fit into circular material systems.

One major area of substitution is bio-based plastics, which are produced from renewable biomass such as corn starch, sugarcane, cellulose, algae, or agricultural waste. These plastics can be designed to be either biodegradable (e.g., polylactic acid—PLA) or durable (e.g., bio-based polyethylene), depending on the application. Bio-based plastics are increasingly used in packaging, disposable cutlery, textiles, and automotive components. However, their sustainability depends on responsible feedstock sourcing, production methods, and end-of-life management.

Bio-based composites combine natural fibers (such as hemp, flax, jute, or bamboo) with biopolymers or resins. These materials offer lightweight, high-strength alternatives to synthetic composites and are used in construction, furniture, electronics, and vehicle interiors. When designed for recyclability or biodegradability, bio-composites can contribute to circular and regenerative product systems.

Bio-lubricants and solvents derived from vegetable oils, tall oil, or fermentation processes provide safer alternatives to petroleum-based industrial chemicals. They are less toxic, biodegradable, and often perform well under harsh conditions. These substitutes are used in manufacturing, maintenance, agriculture, and cleaning industries where pollution prevention is a key concern.

In the chemical sector, bio-based inputs can replace fossil feedstocks in the production of platform chemicals such as succinic acid, acetic acid, ethanol, and lactic acid. These chemicals serve as building blocks for bioplastics, coatings, adhesives, and cosmetics. Advances in synthetic biology and fermentation technologies are enabling more efficient and scalable production of these compounds using engineered microbes and renewable feedstocks.

Textile fibers such as lyocell (from wood pulp), banana fiber, and seaweed-based yarns are emerging alternatives to fossil-derived synthetics like polyester and nylon. These fibers reduce microplastic pollution and can be produced with significantly lower energy and chemical inputs when managed sustainably.

Importantly, not all bio-based alternatives are inherently sustainable. Their environmental profile depends on land use, input requirements, processing emissions, and waste outcomes. For example, diverting food crops to produce bioplastics can compete with food security and drive deforestation, unless mitigated through residue-based or second-generation feedstocks. Therefore, nature-positive bio-based alternatives must be carefully assessed across their lifecycle, prioritize non-food biomass and waste streams, and be compatible with circular reuse, recycling, or composting systems.

In summary, bio-based alternatives present an opportunity to decouple economic activity from fossil resource use. When designed and implemented within a circular, systems-based framework, they offer pathways to materially support climate goals, resource efficiency, and ecosystem regeneration.

Circularity Loops: Reuse, Repair, Remanufacture, Composting, Anaerobic Digestion

A nature-positive circular bioeconomy is built on the principle of maintaining the value of materials for as long as possible while minimizing environmental impacts. This is achieved through a series of circularity loops—strategic pathways that keep products, components, and materials in use, in cycles that mimic or complement natural systems. Key loops include reuse, repair, remanufacture, composting, and anaerobic digestion, each with distinct roles depending on the product type, material properties, and intended lifespan.

Reuse refers to the repeated use of products or components without significant alteration. In the context of bio-based systems, reuse extends the life of items such as wooden pallets, reusable packaging, or bio-composite furniture. Designing for reuse involves ensuring durability, modularity, and easy cleaning or reassembly. This loop reduces demand for new raw materials and lowers energy use associated with reprocessing.

Repair enables the restoration of damaged or malfunctioning products to functional condition. Bio-based products designed for repair incorporate replaceable parts and use fastening methods that allow for easy disassembly. Repair systems are particularly relevant for durable goods like furniture, construction materials, or tools made from timber or natural fiber composites. Facilitating access to spare parts, manuals, and repair services is essential to supporting this loop.

Remanufacture involves recovering used components and restoring them to like-new condition, often with upgrades. This approach is common in industrial machinery, packaging containers, and modular construction components. For bio-based products, remanufacturing can be applied to composite panels, bio-resins, or engineered wood, provided that the materials maintain structural integrity after initial use. This loop allows for high-value retention and reduces waste generation.

Composting is the biological decomposition of organic materials under aerobic conditions, resulting in nutrient-rich humus that can be returned to soils. Composting is suitable for short-lived bio-based products—such as food packaging, agricultural films, or disposable tableware—when these are designed to meet compostability standards and free from contaminants. Composting contributes to soil regeneration, closes nutrient cycles, and reduces landfill methane emissions.

Anaerobic digestion is a process in which microorganisms break down organic matter in oxygen-free environments, producing biogas (a renewable energy source) and digestate (a nutrient-rich soil amendment). This loop is particularly important for managing organic waste streams, such as food waste, crop residues, or sewage sludge. Anaerobic digestion aligns with circular and regenerative goals by simultaneously generating energy and returning nutrients to the land.

Each circularity loop is most effective when aligned with appropriate product design, policy support, and infrastructure availability. Decision-makers must consider the environmental trade-offs and economic feasibility of each loop in specific contexts. For instance, compostable products are beneficial only if industrial composting facilities are available, while repair and remanufacture require product designs that support disassembly and reassembly.

Integrating these circularity loops into bioeconomy strategies ensures that biological materials are cycled efficiently and safely, contributing to reduced waste, lower emissions, and enhanced ecosystem services. Together, these loops form the operational backbone of a circular system that regenerates rather than depletes natural resources.

Enhancing Circularity Through Biorefineries and Cascading Value Chains

Biorefineries and cascading value chains are essential components of a nature-positive circular bioeconomy. They enable the efficient conversion of biomass into a wide range of bio-based products and energy, while maximizing resource use, minimizing waste, and preserving the ecological value of feedstocks. When aligned with circularity principles, these systems create multiple value streams from a single biomass input and extend the functional life of resources across economic sectors.

A biorefinery is a facility that integrates biomass processing technologies to produce a portfolio of products—such as fuels, chemicals, materials, and energy—from renewable biological sources. This concept mirrors the fossil fuel-based refinery but is based on renewable and potentially regenerative inputs. Unlike conventional biomass facilities that produce a single product (e.g., ethanol or biogas), biorefineries extract value in multiple forms, increasing the efficiency and economic viability of biomass utilization.

Biorefineries support circularity by:

- Utilizing diverse feedstocks, including agricultural residues, food waste, forest by-products, and algae
- Prioritizing high-value applications before lower-value energy recovery
- Integrating closed-loop water, nutrient, and energy systems to reduce environmental footprints

33

- Creating synergies between industries through industrial symbiosis, where waste or by-products from one process serve as inputs for another

Cascading value chains further enhance circularity by structuring biomass use in a hierarchy that first allocates it to the highest-value or most resource-efficient applications, before moving it to subsequent uses. This ensures that the full utility of biomass is realized across different stages. For example, wood can be used first in long-life construction materials, then repurposed into panels or furniture, followed by conversion into pulp, and finally used for energy or composting.

This cascading approach has several environmental and economic benefits:

- It reduces pressure on land and ecosystems by maximizing output per unit of biomass
- It delays final disposal or degradation, extending material lifespans
- It reduces emissions associated with premature combustion or degradation of organic matter
- It creates employment and innovation opportunities in multiple sectors, including materials science, bioenergy, and industrial design

To fully implement cascading value chains, supportive policy frameworks are needed that incentivize high-value uses, internalize environmental costs, and disincentivize low-efficiency applications (such as burning raw biomass). Additionally, technological integration within and between facilities is crucial to enable seamless transitions between product stages, supported by traceability systems and quality standards.

In a nature-positive context, biorefineries and cascading chains must be designed to avoid overharvesting, preserve soil and water health, and support biodiversity. This means prioritizing waste and residue streams over virgin biomass, respecting ecological thresholds, and integrating environmental safeguards throughout the value chain.

When properly implemented, biorefineries and cascading use represent powerful tools for decoupling economic development from resource extraction, enabling circular flows that regenerate ecosystems and reduce the overall footprint of biomass-based production systems.

Addressing the Challenges of Contamination, Complexity, and Material Mixing

One of the main barriers to achieving high levels of circularity in bio-based systems is the presence of contamination, material complexity, and mixing of incompatible materials. These factors reduce the quality and recyclability of bio-based products, limit end-of-life options, and increase processing costs. In a nature-positive circular bioeconomy, addressing these challenges is essential to ensure that biological resources can be safely and effectively cycled through multiple uses without generating waste or environmental harm.

Contamination refers to the presence of unwanted substances—such as food residues, synthetic polymers, adhesives, inks, or hazardous chemicals—that compromise the quality of bio-based feedstocks and finished products. Contaminants can make recycling or composting processes inefficient or even infeasible. For example, compostable packaging contaminated with non-compostable plastics or heavy metals can disrupt organic waste streams and produce poor-quality compost. Contamination also limits the safety and reliability of recycled materials for subsequent uses.

To reduce contamination risks, product designers must prioritize clean material inputs, minimize additive use, and avoid chemical treatments that hinder biodegradation or recycling. Clear labelling, user guidance, and harmonized collection systems also play a role in reducing post-consumer contamination. At the processing level, presorting technologies, material identification tools, and quality assurance protocols can enhance feedstock purity and system reliability.

Material complexity presents another obstacle, especially in products made from multiple layers or composite materials. While these materials often offer superior performance (e.g., strength, barrier properties), they are difficult to separate and recycle. Laminates that combine natural fibers with synthetic resins or films, for example, pose major challenges for mechanical recycling or biodegradation. Even when bio-based, such complexity can limit circularity unless specifically designed for separation and reprocessing.

To address this, product developers should follow the principle of design for disassembly, allowing materials to be separated into homogenous streams at the end of their useful life. This includes using mechanical fasteners instead of adhesives, modular design, and reversible joining techniques. When composite materials are necessary, efforts should focus on ensuring that the entire system is recyclable or compostable in existing infrastructure, and that materials are compatible within a closed-loop system.

Material mixing—the unintended or deliberate combination of different materials, especially incompatible ones—further complicates reuse and recycling. In bio-based systems, this often occurs in packaging, textiles, and construction materials, where natural fibers are blended with synthetic polymers, metal foils, or chemical treatments. These mixtures reduce the technical recyclability and may introduce pollutants into organic recycling streams.

Reducing material mixing requires standardization, transparency, and traceability across the value chain. Digital product passports, material registries, and supply chain disclosure tools can help ensure that actors understand what materials are used and how they behave at end-of-life. Policy interventions—such as restrictions on multilayer packaging, incentives for mono-material products, or mandatory labelling—can further discourage problematic material combinations.

In sum, addressing contamination, complexity, and mixing is critical for achieving functional and regenerative circular systems. These challenges must be tackled at the design stage, supported by infrastructure development, and reinforced through governance and consumer behavior. Only by overcoming these barriers can bio-based systems achieve the level of purity, efficiency, and safety required for high-value circularity that benefits both the economy and the environment.

Chapter 4. Enabling Technologies and Digital Tools for Nature-Positive Circularity

Technology plays a pivotal role in advancing a nature-positive circular bioeconomy by enabling more efficient use of biological resources, improving traceability, and supporting regenerative outcomes. Digital tools and biotechnologies allow for better monitoring, design, and optimization of circular systems, helping to close material loops while minimizing ecological impacts.

This chapter explores the enabling technologies that support nature-positive circularity across biomass production, processing, and end-of-life management. It covers advances in biotechnology, synthetic biology, and precision fermentation that create low-impact alternatives to fossil-based materials, as well as biorefinery systems that maximize resource value through cascading use.

The chapter also examines the role of digital innovations—such as artificial intelligence, the Internet of Things, digital twins, blockchain, and sensor networks—in improving system transparency, traceability, and performance. These tools facilitate data-driven decisions, support ecosystem monitoring, and enhance accountability in bio-based value chains.

Together, these technologies provide the infrastructure and intelligence needed to align bioeconomy activities with environmental thresholds and circular economy goals. By focusing on their application in real-world systems, this chapter demonstrates how innovation can drive operational efficiency while contributing to biodiversity conservation, carbon reduction, and the restoration of natural capital.

Role of Biotechnology, Synthetic Biology, and Precision Fermentation

Biotechnology, synthetic biology, and precision fermentation are transformative enablers in the shift toward a nature-positive circular bioeconomy. These tools allow for the development of high-performance bio-based materials, alternative proteins, and green chemicals with significantly lower environmental impacts than their fossil-based or industrially intensive counterparts. When responsibly applied, they offer ways to reduce resource use, diversify biomass inputs, and enhance the functional value of biological processes.

Biotechnology refers broadly to the use of biological systems or organisms to develop products and processes. In the bioeconomy, this includes genetic improvement of crops for higher yields, resistance to pests or drought, and suitability for circular systems (e.g., easier processing, higher-value residues). Biotechnology also supports microbial processing, enzymatic conversion, and metabolic engineering to transform biomass into fuels, bioplastics, and biochemicals. These techniques reduce dependency on fossil inputs and can utilize non-food biomass or waste streams as feedstocks, thereby improving circularity and minimizing competition with food systems.

Synthetic biology builds on traditional biotechnology by enabling the design and construction of entirely new biological parts, systems, or organisms. It allows researchers to program microorganisms— such as bacteria, yeast, or algae—to produce specific molecules or materials with high precision. For example, synthetic biology can be used to engineer microbes that produce spider silk proteins, biodegradable plastics, or rare flavor compounds without the need for intensive land or resource use. These bio-fabricated materials are typically produced in bioreactors, offering controlled environments that limit pollution and land-use pressures.

Precision fermentation is a powerful application of synthetic biology in which genetically engineered microorganisms are used to produce target ingredients, often for food, feed, or cosmetic applications. Unlike traditional fermentation, which yields complex mixtures, precision fermentation is tailored to produce single, purified compounds such as proteins (e.g., casein, whey), enzymes, fats, or

39

pigments. This technology enables the creation of animal-free dairy, sustainable proteins, and specialty bioactives with significantly reduced environmental footprints.

These technologies offer several key benefits for a circular bioeconomy:

- **Feedstock flexibility**: Many engineered microbes can be cultivated on diverse substrates, including waste biomass, agricultural residues, or industrial by-products.
- **Resource efficiency**: Fermentation systems typically require less land and water than conventional agricultural production, helping reduce ecological pressures.
- **High product specificity**: Precision manufacturing reduces the need for intensive downstream processing and chemical refinement, lowering energy and material inputs.
- **Reduced environmental externalities**: Closed-system bioreactors minimize emissions, contamination, and land degradation associated with conventional production.

However, to ensure a nature-positive outcome, the deployment of biotechnology and synthetic biology must be guided by precautionary principles, lifecycle assessments, and sustainability criteria. Risks related to biosafety, gene flow, ecosystem disruption, and ethical considerations must be managed through robust regulation, stakeholder engagement, and transparent governance.

In summary, biotechnology, synthetic biology, and precision fermentation expand the bioeconomy's potential while supporting circularity and regeneration. When strategically integrated, they enable the production of high-value materials with low environmental cost, contributing to climate goals, biodiversity conservation, and sustainable development in a resource-constrained world.

AI and IoT for Biomass Monitoring, Traceability, and Optimization

Artificial Intelligence (AI) and the Internet of Things (IoT) are playing an increasingly important role in enabling the efficient, transparent, and sustainable management of biomass across the value chain. In a nature-positive circular bioeconomy, these digital tools support better decision-making, reduce resource waste, and ensure that biomass production and use align with environmental and regenerative goals. By integrating sensors, data analytics, and automated systems, AI and IoT help close material loops, monitor ecological impacts, and improve supply chain transparency.

IoT technologies involve networks of interconnected sensors and devices that collect and transmit real-time data from physical environments. In biomass systems, IoT is used to monitor variables such as soil moisture, temperature, nutrient levels, crop health, and harvesting status. For example, precision agriculture systems deploy soil sensors, drones, and satellite imagery to optimize input use and timing, enhancing yield while reducing over-fertilization, water consumption, and land degradation. In forestry, IoT-enabled devices track tree growth, detect illegal logging, and support sustainable harvest planning.

In bio-refining and biomass processing facilities, IoT systems monitor flow rates, energy consumption, emissions, and material quality. This enables better process optimization, ensuring that energy, water, and chemicals are used efficiently while minimizing waste. The data collected can also support preventive maintenance of equipment and increase overall system resilience.

AI enhances the value of IoT data through advanced analytics, pattern recognition, and predictive modeling. AI systems can forecast biomass yields, identify disease outbreaks, and recommend optimized harvesting times based on weather patterns, soil conditions, and crop cycles. In logistics, AI-driven platforms can streamline biomass collection, routing, and storage to minimize spoilage and transportation emissions.

One of the most transformative applications of AI and IoT is in traceability and supply chain transparency. Through the integration of sensors, geolocation data, and blockchain technology, biomass flows can be tracked from source to end-product. This allows stakeholders—including regulators, producers, and consumers—to verify sustainability credentials, detect unsustainable practices, and ensure compliance with environmental standards. Traceability systems can confirm that biomass was harvested legally, sourced from non-deforested land, or produced under certified sustainable practices.

For instance, in compostable packaging or bio-based textiles, digital tracking can confirm the origin of feedstocks, processing methods, and environmental attributes. In waste management, smart bins and sensors can track organic waste volumes, contamination levels, and collection patterns, helping municipalities and companies improve circularity metrics and service design.

Despite their potential, AI and IoT applications require investment in digital infrastructure, interoperability, and capacity-building, particularly in rural and emerging economies. Data privacy, cybersecurity, and equitable access to technology must also be addressed to prevent technological disparities and ensure inclusivity.

In conclusion, AI and IoT are key digital enablers of a nature-positive circular bioeconomy. They provide the intelligence and automation needed to optimize resource use, reduce environmental impacts, and build resilient, transparent, and regenerative biomass systems across sectors and scales.

Digital Twins and Blockchain in Circular Supply Chains

Digital twins and blockchain technology are emerging as critical digital tools in the development of transparent, efficient, and accountable circular bioeconomy supply chains. Together, they enable real-time tracking, performance optimization, and data integrity, supporting the design and management of nature-positive value chains that are both circular and regenerative.

A digital twin is a virtual replica of a physical asset, system, or process that is continuously updated using real-world data collected via sensors, IoT devices, and monitoring systems. In biomass supply chains, digital twins can model farms, forests, bio-refineries, transport systems, and even entire production facilities. These models provide real-time insights into operations, resource flows, energy use, and environmental performance, allowing for predictive analytics and scenario testing.

For example, in agriculture or forestry, digital twins can simulate soil health dynamics, crop growth, carbon storage, and biodiversity outcomes under different management practices. This helps stakeholders make informed decisions about harvesting schedules, input use, and restoration efforts. In processing facilities, digital twins can be used to optimize biorefinery operations, minimize downtime, and improve waste valorization efficiency.

From a circularity perspective, digital twins are valuable for modeling the lifecycle of bio-based products, identifying inefficiencies, and enabling circular design improvements. By visualizing flows of materials, energy, and emissions, they support more effective decision-making around reuse, remanufacture, or recycling strategies.

Blockchain provides a decentralized and tamper-proof ledger for recording transactions and data exchanges across supply chains. In the circular bioeconomy, blockchain ensures the traceability, transparency, and verification of biomass origins, processing methods, and sustainability claims. Each stage of the supply chain—from raw material production to final product disposal—can be logged as a secure, immutable data point.

For instance, a blockchain-based system can verify that wood used in a bio-based product comes from sustainably managed forests, or that compostable packaging is processed in a certified facility. Smart contracts embedded in the blockchain can automate compliance with sustainability criteria, release payments only when environmental thresholds are met, or trigger alerts when irregularities occur.

When combined, digital twins and blockchain enhance supply chain governance in several ways:

- **End-to-end visibility**: Stakeholders can track products and materials throughout their lifecycle with high resolution and credibility.
- **Risk reduction**: Early detection of supply chain disruptions, fraud, or unsustainable practices becomes possible.
- **Performance optimization**: Continuous data feedback from digital twins can be linked with blockchain records to verify improvements in resource efficiency, emissions, or biodiversity impact.
- **Credible reporting**: Companies can provide verified environmental performance data to regulators, financiers, and consumers, supporting ESG disclosures and certification schemes.

Adopting these technologies does require overcoming challenges such as data standardization, interoperability, costs of implementation, and digital literacy. However, as technology becomes more accessible, the combined power of digital twins and blockchain can drive a step-change in how circular bioeconomy supply chains are managed—shifting from reactive monitoring to predictive, verified, and regenerative systems.

In summary, digital twins and blockchain together offer the digital backbone for managing complex circular systems. They ensure that bio-based production is not only efficient and low-impact but also verifiably sustainable, enabling trust and collaboration across the nature-positive circular bioeconomy.

Material Flow Analysis and Lifecycle Tools for Regenerative Planning

Material Flow Analysis (MFA) and lifecycle assessment (LCA) are essential analytical tools for enabling regenerative planning within the nature-positive circular bioeconomy. These tools help quantify material and energy use across systems, identify inefficiencies and hotspots, and evaluate environmental impacts. When applied with a regeneration-focused lens, MFA and LCA can support decision-making that not only minimizes harm but actively contributes to ecosystem restoration and long-term sustainability.

MFA tracks the physical flows of materials into, through, and out of a defined system over time. In the bioeconomy, MFA can be used to analyze biomass sourcing, transformation, use, and disposal. It helps identify where materials are lost, underutilized, or wasted, enabling targeted interventions to increase circularity and value retention.

For example, MFA can assess:

- The quantity and type of biomass entering a production facility
- The conversion efficiency of biomass into bio-based products
- Waste streams and by-products that could be valorized (e.g., digestate from biogas plants)
- Leakages that result in environmental degradation (e.g., runoff from agricultural systems)

By providing a system-wide overview, MFA allows planners and policymakers to understand resource dependencies, evaluate circularity potential, and align bio-based systems with regional ecological capacities.

Lifecycle Assessment (LCA) evaluates the environmental impacts associated with all stages of a product's life—from raw material extraction to end-of-life. This includes metrics such as greenhouse gas emissions, water use, energy demand, land occupation, eutrophication, and impacts on biodiversity. In the context of a regenerative circular bioeconomy, LCA is extended beyond carbon footprints to assess ecosystem health, soil regeneration, and biodiversity enhancement.

A regenerative LCA approach includes:

- Assessment of positive ecological outcomes, such as improved soil organic carbon or habitat restoration
- Inclusion of nature-positive indicators, not just harm reduction (e.g., net gain in biodiversity rather than reduced loss)
- Integration of temporal and spatial factors, acknowledging that impacts vary over time and across ecosystems
- Differentiation between linear, circular, and regenerative systems, offering a comparative lens for evaluating system design choices

Together, MFA and LCA help identify the most sustainable and regenerative pathways for biomass use, comparing trade-offs among different uses (e.g., food vs. fuel vs. materials) and technologies (e.g., composting vs. anaerobic digestion). They also provide the empirical foundation for policy frameworks, eco-labelling, and corporate sustainability disclosures, ensuring that claims of circularity or nature-positivity are backed by robust evidence.

For effective regenerative planning, these tools must be applied iteratively and collaboratively—engaging stakeholders across sectors, integrating local ecological data, and aligning with global sustainability standards. Increasingly, digital platforms are making MFA and LCA more accessible, enabling real-time modelling and integration with technologies like AI, IoT, and blockchain.

In summary, MFA and LCA offer a critical lens through which the circular bioeconomy can move from efficiency-focused design to truly regenerative outcomes. By grounding planning in quantifiable data and ecological performance, these tools help ensure that biomass systems contribute positively to both human prosperity and planetary health.

Sensor-Driven Systems for Biodiversity Impact Measurement

In a nature-positive circular bioeconomy, the ability to monitor, quantify, and respond to biodiversity impacts is essential. Sensor-driven systems provide the technological foundation for achieving this, offering real-time, high-resolution data on ecological conditions across landscapes, production systems, and supply chains. These systems enhance transparency, support adaptive management, and ensure that biomass sourcing, processing, and product development align with biodiversity protection and regeneration goals.

Sensor technologies—including terrestrial, aerial, and aquatic sensors—can measure a wide range of biodiversity-relevant indicators, such as species presence and abundance, vegetation cover, habitat condition, soil health, and water quality. These systems are deployed in forests, agricultural landscapes, wetlands, and coastal zones to track how biomass-related activities affect ecosystem integrity over time.

Key sensor-driven tools include:

- **Acoustic sensors (ecoacoustics):** These detect animal calls and other natural sounds to assess species richness and behavioral changes, particularly in birds, amphibians, and insects. Patterns in soundscapes can indicate habitat disturbance, species displacement, or ecosystem recovery.
- **Camera traps and image recognition:** Motion-activated cameras, coupled with AI-based species identification software, monitor wildlife activity and biodiversity trends. These tools are increasingly used in forests, plantations, and conservation areas linked to biomass production.
- **Soil sensors:** These measure parameters such as soil moisture, temperature, nutrient levels, and microbial

activity—proxies for soil biodiversity and ecosystem health. Healthy soils with diverse biological communities support resilient biomass production systems.

- **Aerial drones and remote sensing:** Equipped with multispectral and thermal sensors, drones and satellites monitor land use, vegetation patterns, and habitat fragmentation. They provide scalable insights into the ecological impacts of land conversion, deforestation, or restoration associated with bio-based supply chains.
- **eDNA (environmental DNA) sensors:** These detect genetic material from organisms in soil, water, or air samples, allowing for non-invasive monitoring of biodiversity across taxa, including rare or cryptic species. eDNA can reveal changes in species composition due to biomass harvesting or land management practices.

Sensor-driven systems offer several benefits in a circular bioeconomy context:

- Timely detection of ecosystem degradation or stress, enabling corrective actions before irreversible damage occurs
- Verification of biodiversity gains in regenerative projects or supply chain sustainability claims
- Support for certification schemes and environmental disclosures through credible, continuous data
- Improved landscape-level planning, allowing for zoning and spatial optimization of biomass activities to avoid ecologically sensitive areas

However, effective use of sensor systems requires data integration, interdisciplinary expertise, and governance frameworks to ensure ethical use, data privacy, and equitable access. It is also important to pair sensor outputs with context-specific ecological interpretation, recognizing that biodiversity responses are complex and location-dependent.

In conclusion, sensor-driven biodiversity monitoring enhances the ability of bioeconomy actors to operate within ecological boundaries. By embedding these technologies into supply chains and land-use planning, a nature-positive circular bioeconomy can move from intention to measurable outcomes—ensuring that economic regeneration goes hand-in-hand with ecological renewal.

Emerging Innovations in Nutrient Recovery and Biowaste Valorization

The nature-positive circular bioeconomy depends on efficient nutrient cycling and the full utilization of biowaste streams to reduce environmental pressure and regenerate ecosystems. Emerging innovations in nutrient recovery and biowaste valorization are transforming organic waste from a liability into a valuable resource, closing nutrient loops and enabling the production of renewable energy, fertilizers, materials, and bio-based chemicals. These technologies contribute to resource efficiency, reduce greenhouse gas emissions, and help mitigate nutrient pollution in soil and water systems.

One key area of innovation is advanced anaerobic digestion (AD) systems that not only produce biogas but also improve the recovery and stabilization of nutrients such as nitrogen, phosphorus, and potassium. Modern AD facilities use thermal hydrolysis, membrane separation, or chemical precipitation technologies to extract concentrated fertilizer products from digestate. These nutrients can be reintroduced into agricultural systems, reducing dependence on synthetic fertilizers and enhancing soil fertility.

Struvite precipitation is a promising method for phosphorus recovery from wastewater, digestate, or livestock effluent. By controlling pH and adding magnesium, phosphorus can be recovered as struvite (magnesium ammonium phosphate), a slow-release fertilizer that reduces nutrient runoff and eutrophication risks. Struvite production is increasingly integrated into wastewater treatment plants and agri-industrial operations.

Biochar production through pyrolysis of organic waste is gaining attention for its dual role in nutrient management and carbon sequestration. Biochar retains nutrients, improves soil structure, enhances water retention, and acts as a long-term carbon sink. Innovations in feedstock pre-treatment, kiln design, and biochar activation are increasing its performance and applicability across various soil types and farming systems.

Hydrothermal carbonization (HTC) and supercritical water oxidation (SCWO) are emerging thermochemical processes that convert wet organic waste—such as sewage sludge or food waste—into solid biochar-like materials, nutrient-rich liquids, and heat. These technologies are particularly suited for decentralized applications and regions lacking conventional waste treatment infrastructure.

Microbial consortia and synthetic biology are enabling more targeted and efficient breakdown of complex organic matter into specific high-value products. Engineered microbes are being developed to convert biowaste into bioplastics (e.g., polyhydroxyalkanoates), enzymes, and biosurfactants. Such innovations add economic value to waste streams and diversify the portfolio of bio-based materials derived from organic waste.

Nutrient recovery from blackwater and urine-diverting systems is another frontier. Decentralized sanitation technologies, including vacuum toilets and source-separating systems, enable the capture and treatment of human waste streams at the household or community level. Innovations in electrochemical separation and biological treatment allow recovery of clean water, fertilizers, and even energy in compact, closed-loop systems.

Digital platforms and smart sensors are enhancing the traceability and quality control of biowaste feedstocks, supporting safe and standardized valorization pathways. Sensors monitor nutrient content, contamination levels, and processing conditions, ensuring that outputs meet regulatory and agronomic standards.

For these innovations to achieve scale and impact, enabling conditions are necessary:

- Clear regulatory frameworks that define quality standards for recovered nutrients and biowaste-derived products
- Incentives and market mechanisms that promote nutrient circularity, such as subsidies, carbon credits, or ecolabels
- Infrastructure investment and cross-sector collaboration, particularly between municipalities, agriculture, and industry

In summary, nutrient recovery and biowaste valorization technologies are central to transforming organic waste into solutions for food security, soil health, climate resilience, and pollution prevention. These emerging innovations reinforce the regenerative potential of the circular bioeconomy by turning waste into wealth— economically, ecologically, and socially.

Chapter 5. Financing Nature-Positive Circular Bioeconomy Transitions

Scaling a nature-positive circular bioeconomy requires strategic investment and financial mechanisms that support regenerative practices, circular infrastructure, and bio-based innovation. Traditional financing models often prioritize short-term returns and linear growth, which can limit the flow of capital into systems that emphasize ecological restoration, material circularity, and long-term resilience.

This chapter explores the financial tools, investment frameworks, and public policy interventions needed to enable circular bioeconomy transitions. It outlines the role of green bonds, sustainability-linked loans, blended finance, and natural capital accounting in channeling resources toward regenerative outcomes. It also examines how venture capital and private equity are evolving to support scalable bio-based solutions that operate within planetary boundaries.

The chapter highlights the importance of de-risking early-stage innovation, reforming environmentally harmful subsidies, and aligning public procurement with circular and bioeconomy objectives. In addition, it discusses the integration of science-based and nature-positive indicators into financing criteria to ensure that investments drive measurable environmental and social benefits.

By linking finance to ecological and circular performance, this chapter emphasizes the need for a systemic shift in how value is defined and capital is allocated. It shows how well-designed financial strategies can accelerate the transition to regenerative, inclusive, and resilient bioeconomy systems.

Investment Principles Aligned with Regenerative and Circular Objectives

Financing a nature-positive circular bioeconomy requires a shift from traditional, growth-oriented investment models toward approaches that prioritize long-term ecological resilience, social equity, and material circularity. Investment principles aligned with regenerative and circular objectives are designed to ensure that capital flows support the restoration of natural systems, efficient use of biological resources, and inclusive economic outcomes.

One key principle is long-term value creation. Investors are encouraged to move beyond short-term financial returns and instead assess the broader system-level benefits of their investments, such as improved soil health, reduced waste, biodiversity enhancement, and strengthened local economies. This perspective promotes funding for projects and enterprises that regenerate natural capital and support sustainable livelihoods.

Another guiding principle is risk-adjusted sustainability. This approach integrates environmental, social, and governance (ESG) risks into investment decisions, particularly those related to climate, biodiversity, and supply chain dependencies. By assessing risks such as resource scarcity, land degradation, or regulatory changes, investors can support business models that are more resilient and adaptable in the face of global sustainability challenges.

Circular and regenerative investment also calls for lifecycle thinking. Capital should flow toward enterprises that design products and systems for reuse, repair, recycling, and biological regeneration. Investments in closed-loop infrastructure, biorefineries, and eco-innovation platforms help reduce reliance on virgin resources and externalize fewer environmental costs.

An important principle is alignment with science-based targets. Investors are increasingly expected to support companies and projects that operate within planetary boundaries and have measurable commitments to climate and biodiversity goals. This includes the use of indicators such as carbon intensity, land-use change, and water stewardship to evaluate project performance and impact.

Equity and inclusiveness are also essential. Investments should be structured to support equitable access to financing, particularly for small and medium-sized enterprises (SMEs), cooperatives, and community-led initiatives in the bioeconomy. Regenerative models often emerge from localized, context-specific knowledge, and enabling their growth requires financial mechanisms that are accessible, patient, and responsive to diverse needs.

Transparency and accountability underpin all investment principles. Clear reporting on environmental and social outcomes, open access to data, and third-party verification of impact claims are necessary to build trust and credibility in the investment ecosystem. Investors may adopt tools such as impact-weighted accounting, sustainability-linked finance, or blended finance structures to monitor and communicate performance.

In summary, investment aligned with regenerative and circular objectives emphasizes systems thinking, long-term ecological health, and inclusive development. By adopting these principles, investors play a pivotal role in accelerating the transition to a bioeconomy that is economically viable, environmentally restorative, and socially beneficial.

Green and Sustainable Finance Instruments: Bonds, Loans, and Blended Finance

To accelerate the development of a nature-positive circular bioeconomy, a growing suite of green and sustainable finance instruments is being deployed. These tools mobilize capital by aligning investment flows with environmental and social objectives, offering flexibility for both public and private actors to support regenerative and circular initiatives across sectors. Among the most relevant instruments are green bonds, sustainability-linked loans, and blended finance mechanisms.

Green bonds are fixed-income securities specifically earmarked to fund environmentally beneficial projects. In the context of the circular bioeconomy, proceeds from green bonds can be used to finance sustainable biomass production, biorefineries, composting infrastructure, waste-to-energy systems, or nutrient recovery technologies. Issuers—such as governments, municipalities, or corporations—commit to using the funds for eligible green activities and are typically required to report on impact metrics. Market standards, including the Green Bond Principles and the EU Green Bond Standard, guide issuers in defining and verifying project alignment with environmental goals.

Sustainability-linked loans (SLLs) are another flexible instrument that ties borrowing terms—such as interest rates—to the borrower's achievement of predetermined sustainability performance targets. These targets may include reductions in emissions, water use, or material waste, or improvements in circularity metrics such as product recyclability or resource efficiency. Unlike green bonds, which require use-of-proceeds restrictions, SLLs offer general-purpose financing while incentivizing performance improvements through measurable environmental outcomes.

Blended finance leverages public or philanthropic capital to de-risk private investment in projects that may be perceived as too risky or uncertain in the early stages. In the circular bioeconomy, blended finance structures can support the development of pilot projects, scale innovative technologies, or build capacity in underserved markets. For example, concessional loans or first-loss guarantees from public institutions can make it more attractive for commercial investors to participate in regenerative agriculture initiatives or organic waste valorization programs.

Other emerging instruments include sustainability-linked bonds, transition bonds, and results-based finance. Each offers a way to align financial returns with circular and regenerative goals, provided that the underlying metrics and monitoring frameworks are credible, transparent, and robust.

For these instruments to be effective, enabling conditions must be in place. This includes harmonized taxonomies that define what qualifies as circular or nature-positive investment, standardized reporting protocols, and third-party verification of environmental and social performance. Access to reliable data and technical assistance for project developers—especially in the agriculture, forestry, and waste sectors—is also critical to scaling finance flows.

In summary, green and sustainable finance instruments provide diverse pathways to mobilize capital for circular bioeconomy solutions. When well-designed and transparently implemented, they can support innovation, reduce risk, and channel investment toward activities that contribute meaningfully to climate goals, biodiversity protection, and ecosystem restoration.

Monetizing Biodiversity and Ecosystem Services Through Natural Capital Accounting

Natural capital accounting is an emerging tool that helps quantify, value, and integrate nature's contributions into financial and policy decision-making. By capturing the economic value of biodiversity and ecosystem services, it provides a structured approach to aligning circular bioeconomy investments with ecological sustainability and long-term value creation.

Ecosystem services—such as pollination, soil fertility, water purification, and climate regulation—are foundational to biomass production and resource regeneration. However, these services are often invisible in conventional accounting systems, leading to underinvestment in conservation and degradation of ecological assets. Natural capital accounting addresses this gap by incorporating nature's value into national accounts, corporate balance sheets, and project assessments.

The process typically involves identifying natural assets (e.g., forests, wetlands, soils), quantifying their condition and services, and assigning monetary or non-monetary values to these flows. Methods range from market pricing and cost-based valuation to more complex models such as contingent valuation or benefit transfer. These valuations can inform budgeting, land-use planning, and investment strategies in the bioeconomy.

In a circular bioeconomy context, natural capital accounting supports the internalization of environmental costs and benefits. For example, it can reveal the avoided costs of water treatment resulting from wetland restoration, or the value of carbon sequestration provided by regenerative agriculture. These insights can be used to design incentive structures such as payments for ecosystem services (PES), biodiversity credits, or conservation-linked financing mechanisms.

At the corporate level, natural capital assessments help companies understand their dependencies and impacts on ecosystems. This enables the identification of material risks and opportunities related to biodiversity and resource use. Companies engaged in biomass sourcing or bio-based production can use natural capital data to guide sourcing decisions, improve supply chain sustainability, and strengthen environmental disclosures.

Governments and financial institutions are increasingly using natural capital accounts to support evidence-based policy and investment. The System of Environmental-Economic Accounting (SEEA) framework, developed by the United Nations, is being adopted by countries to measure the contribution of ecosystems to national economies and to track progress toward sustainability goals.

Natural capital accounting does not imply commodifying nature in a simplistic sense. Rather, it provides a framework for recognizing the real economic implications of ecological change and for embedding environmental integrity in decision-making. When used appropriately, it can help direct financial and policy support toward regenerative practices, prevent ecological overshoot, and reinforce the role of biodiversity and ecosystems as integral components of the bioeconomy.

Role of Public Finance, Subsidies Reform, and Fiscal Incentives

Public finance plays a pivotal role in establishing the enabling environment for a nature-positive circular bioeconomy. Through targeted expenditure, fiscal policy, and regulatory frameworks, governments can support early-stage innovation, de-risk private investment, and drive systemic changes in production and consumption patterns. When aligned with circular and regenerative objectives, public finance mechanisms can correct market failures, internalize environmental externalities, and ensure equitable access to opportunities in the bioeconomy.

Direct public investment in infrastructure, research, and development is essential to scale up circular systems for biomass use, biowaste processing, nutrient recovery, and sustainable land management. National and local governments can fund demonstration projects, technology incubators, and pilot programs that test new circular models or support knowledge transfer. Public procurement policies can also stimulate demand for certified bio-based and circular products by prioritizing sustainability criteria in purchasing decisions.

Subsidies reform is another critical area. Many current subsidy regimes promote linear and extractive models by lowering the cost of fossil fuels, synthetic fertilizers, monoculture production, or waste disposal. These subsidies often create disincentives for circular and regenerative alternatives. Reforming or phasing out harmful subsidies can level the playing field and reduce ecological pressures. Redirected subsidies can then be used to support practices such as regenerative agriculture, composting, agroforestry, and sustainable forest management.

Fiscal incentives, including tax credits, accelerated depreciation, and grants, can encourage investment in circular bioeconomy infrastructure and technologies. For instance, tax relief can be provided for businesses that invest in biorefineries, use certified sustainable biomass, or develop recyclable or compostable packaging. Reduced value-added tax (VAT) on refurbished bio-based goods or composting services can help shift consumer behavior and reduce waste generation.

Governments may also offer results-based financing or matching grants to reward measurable improvements in biodiversity, emissions reductions, or waste diversion. These tools can be tied to nature-positive indicators and used to support landscape-scale restoration efforts, integrated land-use planning, or circular economy clusters.

To maximize effectiveness, public finance should be coordinated across ministries and levels of government, and aligned with national circular economy strategies, climate goals, and biodiversity commitments. Transparency, clear eligibility criteria, and robust monitoring frameworks are necessary to ensure that public funds deliver real environmental and social outcomes.

The strategic use of public finance, combined with subsidy reform and well-designed fiscal incentives, can accelerate the transition to a circular bioeconomy that regenerates ecosystems, creates green jobs, and builds resilience across sectors.

Venture Capital and Private Equity in Bio-Based Innovation

Venture capital (VC) and private equity (PE) play a vital role in advancing bio-based innovation within a nature-positive circular bioeconomy. These sources of private financing are particularly important for scaling early- and growth-stage enterprises that develop new technologies, materials, and business models aligned with circularity and regeneration. By providing not only capital but also strategic guidance, VC and PE investors help bridge the gap between research, commercialization, and market adoption.

Venture capital is well-suited for high-risk, high-reward investments in innovative bio-based startups. This includes firms developing novel bioplastics, fermentation-derived materials, bio-based textiles, compostable packaging, and alternative proteins. These ventures often rely on synthetic biology, biomimicry, or biorefinery platforms to disrupt traditional value chains. VC funding enables rapid iteration, pilot-scale development, and the recruitment of skilled teams needed to bring new solutions to market.

Private equity investors tend to engage at later stages, supporting the expansion or consolidation of companies that have demonstrated commercial viability. In the circular bioeconomy, PE may focus on scaling bioproduct manufacturers, aggregating organic waste management firms, or investing in integrated bioeconomy clusters. These investors often contribute operational expertise and performance management to help companies achieve growth while improving resource efficiency and environmental outcomes.

To align with regenerative and circular objectives, VC and PE firms are increasingly adopting impact investing frameworks. These frameworks evaluate investments not only by financial return but also by measurable environmental and social performance. Criteria may include emissions reduction, material circularity, biodiversity impact, and inclusion of smallholders or underserved communities in supply chains.

Investors are also seeking opportunities that integrate multiple value streams, such as platforms that convert agricultural residues into bioplastics and energy while sequestering carbon and restoring soil. Such integrated models reflect the systems thinking required in a nature-positive bioeconomy and can yield diversified revenue sources, reducing financial risk.

Challenges remain, particularly around the long time horizons and infrastructure dependencies associated with bio-based ventures. Many innovations require access to reliable biomass supplies, industrial-scale processing facilities, and supportive policy environments. Investors must conduct rigorous due diligence to assess technology readiness, feedstock sustainability, and regulatory exposure.

Blended finance arrangements can enhance the attractiveness of VC and PE in this space by using public or philanthropic capital to absorb early-stage risk. This encourages greater private sector participation in markets that might otherwise be overlooked due to uncertainty or perceived complexity.

As sustainability-driven innovation becomes more central to economic transformation, venture capital and private equity are expected to play an increasingly prominent role. Their ability to catalyze change, accelerate technology deployment, and support scalable business models positions them as key enablers of the circular bioeconomy transition.

Risk Mitigation and Scaling Models for Bio-Circular Startups

Bio-circular startups face a unique set of risks that can hinder their ability to grow and compete in mainstream markets. These risks range from feedstock variability and uncertain regulatory environments to high upfront capital requirements, long development cycles, and limited infrastructure. To navigate these challenges and achieve scale, startups must adopt tailored risk mitigation strategies and business models that support resilience, flexibility, and long-term viability.

One key approach is de-risking through feedstock diversification. Bio-circular startups often rely on specific types of organic waste or biomass, which may be seasonal, geographically constrained, or subject to quality fluctuations. Securing access to multiple feedstock sources, including agricultural residues, municipal biowaste, or industrial by-products, reduces dependency on a single stream and increases supply stability. Building partnerships with waste generators and farmers can also help guarantee consistent input flow and improve traceability.

Technology risk can be mitigated through modular and scalable system design. Rather than deploying capital-intensive, centralized facilities from the outset, startups can use pilot-scale units or mobile processing platforms to test and refine their technologies in real-world settings. This staged deployment allows for continuous learning, cost control, and easier adaptation to different regional contexts.

Collaborative models such as industrial symbiosis and platform ecosystems can enhance efficiency and reduce infrastructure risks. Startups co-locating within bioeconomy clusters or eco-industrial parks benefit from shared logistics, utilities, and access to complementary partners for nutrient recovery, material reuse, or energy generation. Such arrangements can improve unit economics and accelerate learning curves through knowledge exchange.

Access to finance is often a bottleneck for scaling. Blended finance models, which combine concessional funding with private capital, can help reduce perceived investment risk. Public grants or first-loss guarantees can make early-stage ventures more attractive to commercial lenders or impact investors. Additionally, performance-based financing (e.g. milestone-linked disbursements) aligns capital inflow with measurable outcomes, providing accountability while easing cash flow challenges.

Startups can further mitigate market risk by targeting niche applications where circular and regenerative features add tangible value. This may include high-margin sectors such as green construction materials, bio-based packaging with compostability claims, or alternative proteins with strong sustainability credentials. Positioning around functionality and environmental performance allows for premium pricing and early market traction.

To scale effectively, startups should develop adaptive go-to-market strategies that accommodate regulatory variation and consumer behavior across regions. Engaging early with policymakers, certification bodies, and waste management authorities helps anticipate compliance requirements and shape a favorable policy environment. Participating in voluntary standards or pilot programs can also build credibility and increase access to procurement channels.

Lastly, investing in data collection and impact measurement strengthens a startup's ability to communicate value to investors, partners, and customers. Tracking circularity metrics, carbon footprint, and biodiversity impacts supports transparency and aligns with growing demands for ESG performance in procurement and financing.

By combining these risk mitigation strategies with scalable and collaborative models, bio-circular startups can enhance resilience and unlock pathways to growth. Their ability to deliver both environmental and economic returns positions them as important drivers in the broader transition to a regenerative circular bioeconomy.

Chapter 6. Policy, Regulatory, and Institutional Frameworks

Policy, regulation, and institutional alignment are central to enabling and scaling a nature-positive circular bioeconomy. While circularity and bio-based innovation have gained traction globally, fragmented or conflicting policies can undermine efforts to regenerate ecosystems, reduce waste, and support inclusive economic transformation. Coherent frameworks are needed to align incentives, manage trade-offs, and ensure that circular bioeconomy systems operate within ecological limits.

This chapter examines the governance mechanisms required to steer the transition toward nature-positive outcomes. It explores how legal tools—such as product standards, eco-labelling, extended producer responsibility, and land-use regulation—can support sustainable biomass use, material recovery, and biodiversity protection. It also discusses the role of science-based targets, tax incentives, and subsidies reform in shifting markets toward circularity and regeneration.

Attention is given to institutional coordination across sectors—especially agriculture, environment, industry, and innovation—as well as the importance of mainstreaming circular bioeconomy principles into national planning, trade policies, and international agreements. Mechanisms for stakeholder participation and transparency are also addressed, supporting legitimacy and long-term policy coherence.

By establishing a supportive regulatory environment and cross-sectoral alignment, this chapter highlights how policy can drive the systems-level change needed to integrate circularity, regeneration, and equity into economic development strategies.

Aligning Bioeconomy, Circular Economy, and Biodiversity Policies

Policy coherence is essential for the effective implementation of a nature-positive circular bioeconomy. Although bioeconomy, circular economy, and biodiversity strategies often share overarching sustainability goals, they are frequently developed and implemented in silos. Aligning these policy domains ensures that biomass use supports regeneration, material efficiency contributes to ecological resilience, and conservation efforts are integrated into economic planning.

Bioeconomy policies generally focus on the sustainable production and use of biological resources for energy, materials, chemicals, and food. These strategies often aim to enhance rural development, technological innovation, and resource security. However, without clear environmental safeguards, bioeconomy policies can lead to increased pressure on land, water, and ecosystems.

Circular economy policies are designed to reduce waste and keep materials in use through strategies like reuse, recycling, and product redesign. While these policies are effective at reducing linear resource flows, they may not always address the specific ecological impacts of biomass production or the protection of natural habitats.

Biodiversity policies, such as those under the Convention on Biological Diversity and the Kunming-Montreal Global Biodiversity Framework, aim to conserve ecosystems, species, and genetic diversity. These policies prioritize protected areas, ecological restoration, and sustainable land management, but may not always intersect with economic development strategies unless explicitly linked.

To align these three agendas, governments and institutions can adopt integrated frameworks that incorporate circular and regenerative principles into bioeconomy planning, while embedding biodiversity goals into circular economy strategies. This requires shared metrics, cross-sector coordination, and mechanisms to manage trade-offs.

Policy alignment can be facilitated by:

- Developing national strategies that explicitly link bioeconomy and circular economy objectives with biodiversity conservation targets
- Embedding nature-positive criteria into funding programs for circular bioeconomy innovation and infrastructure
- Establishing cross-ministerial task forces or coordination units that bring together agriculture, industry, environment, and finance departments
- Using spatial planning tools that identify areas for biomass production, biodiversity protection, and circular infrastructure development in a coordinated manner
- Harmonizing regulatory standards for sustainable biomass sourcing, compostability, recyclability, and biodiversity safeguards across product value chains

Regulatory instruments such as environmental impact assessments, sustainability certifications, and extended producer responsibility schemes can be designed to serve multiple policy goals. Likewise, indicators such as ecosystem condition, circularity rate, and regenerative land use can provide common reference points for evaluation and reporting.

Aligning bioeconomy, circular economy, and biodiversity policies ensures that economic activities not only reduce harm but actively contribute to environmental recovery and long-term resilience. This integrated approach supports the systemic transformation required to address the interlinked challenges of climate change, biodiversity loss, and unsustainable resource use.

Legal Tools to Promote Bio-Based Products and Restrict Harmful Practices

Legal tools are essential for guiding the transition toward a nature-positive circular bioeconomy. They can incentivize the development and adoption of bio-based products while phasing out materials and practices that contribute to environmental degradation. Through a combination of regulatory standards, bans, mandates, and market-based instruments, legal frameworks help reshape supply chains and consumer behavior in support of circular and regenerative objectives.

One widely used legal mechanism is the establishment of product standards and labeling requirements for bio-based goods. Governments can define criteria for bio-based content, biodegradability, compostability, and recyclability, ensuring that claims are credible and comparable across markets. Standards aligned with international norms (such as ISO or EN) help facilitate trade while giving producers and consumers confidence in environmental performance. Mandatory or voluntary eco-labels further support market uptake by signaling compliance with sustainability benchmarks.

Public procurement laws can be designed to prioritize environmentally preferable products, including those that are bio-based and circular. By requiring public institutions to purchase products that meet defined bio-based criteria, governments can create stable demand, support domestic innovation, and lower market entry barriers for new materials.

Regulatory bans and restrictions are powerful tools to remove harmful materials and practices from the market. For instance, several jurisdictions have banned or restricted single-use plastics, microplastics, or non-compostable packaging, creating space for sustainable bio-based alternatives. Such bans must be carefully designed to avoid unintended consequences, such as increased land-use pressure or substitution with other problematic materials.

Extended producer responsibility (EPR) regulations require producers to take responsibility for the environmental impacts of their products throughout the lifecycle. EPR schemes can be tailored to encourage design for circularity, ensure the recovery of bio-based materials, and hold manufacturers accountable for post-consumer waste. These laws are particularly relevant for packaging, textiles, and electronics that increasingly include bio-based components.

Tax incentives and penalties can steer market behavior by altering the cost structure of competing materials and processes. Reduced taxes on certified bio-based products, or environmental levies on fossil-based or non-recyclable goods, help shift consumption toward circular and regenerative options. These legal tools must be aligned with clear definitions and sustainability safeguards to avoid greenwashing.

Land-use and environmental permitting laws can be used to regulate biomass production, ensuring that bioeconomy development does not lead to deforestation, habitat loss, or ecosystem degradation. Permits can include conditions related to biodiversity protection, soil health, and sustainable harvesting practices. Legal frameworks may also designate specific zones for bio-based industrial activity, balancing economic and ecological priorities.

Trade regulations and border measures can support a level playing field for sustainable products. By establishing import standards for bio-based content or banning products with unsustainable attributes (such as illegally harvested timber or non-degradable plastic), governments can extend the reach of domestic legal frameworks to global supply chains.

The effectiveness of legal tools depends on enforcement, monitoring capacity, and clarity of definitions. Coordination across ministries—particularly environment, agriculture, industry, and trade—is essential to ensure consistency and avoid regulatory gaps. When implemented with transparency and stakeholder engagement, legal tools provide the backbone for a policy environment that supports innovation, protects ecosystems, and advances a sustainable circular bioeconomy.

Extended Producer Responsibility (EPR) and Eco-Labelling

EPR and eco-labelling are two important regulatory and market-based instruments that support the transition to a nature-positive circular bioeconomy. They influence product design, material selection, and consumer behavior, while encouraging producers to take greater responsibility for the environmental impacts of their products throughout their life cycle.

EPR is a policy approach that assigns producers responsibility for the collection, treatment, and disposal of their products once they reach end-of-life. By shifting the financial and operational burden from governments and consumers to producers, EPR incentivizes the design of more durable, repairable, recyclable, and biodegradable products. In the context of bio-based goods, EPR can help ensure that materials such as compostable packaging, biodegradable utensils, and bio-based textiles are properly managed within appropriate recovery systems.

Effective EPR schemes are typically based on clear performance targets, reporting requirements, and differentiated fee structures. Producers of more sustainable or circular products may pay lower fees, while those whose products are harder to recycle or pose environmental risks may face higher charges. This fee modulation encourages upstream innovation and rewards circular design. EPR programs can also fund the development of collection infrastructure for organic and bio-based waste streams, facilitating composting, anaerobic digestion, or material recovery.

Eco-labelling complements EPR by providing consumers and businesses with information about the environmental attributes of products. Labels that certify bio-based content, compostability, recyclability, or sustainability of biomass sourcing help buyers make informed choices and support market differentiation for environmentally preferable goods. Examples include certifications for compostable materials, organic farming standards, or labels indicating renewable resource content.

Eco-labelling schemes must be based on clear criteria, transparent verification processes, and alignment with existing standards. Labels that are widely recognized and third-party verified carry more credibility and can influence procurement decisions in both public and private sectors. In a circular bioeconomy, labels that indicate full life cycle impacts or regenerative qualities—such as soil health, biodiversity impact, or climate benefits—may also emerge as new tools for signaling deeper sustainability performance.

Together, EPR and eco-labelling reinforce one another. EPR drives improvements in product design and waste management systems, while eco-labels influence demand and reward sustainable production. When coordinated within broader policy frameworks, these instruments can help reduce waste, improve material circularity, and strengthen accountability across bio-based value chains. They are essential tools for aligning product innovation with ecological regeneration and responsible consumption.

International Conventions, Trade Policies, and Cross-Border Governance

A nature-positive circular bioeconomy operates across national borders through global supply chains, trade in bio-based products, and shared ecosystems. As such, international conventions, trade policies, and cross-border governance mechanisms are essential for ensuring that biomass sourcing, processing, and product circulation are consistent with environmental sustainability, biodiversity protection, and equitable economic development.

International environmental conventions provide foundational principles and frameworks that influence national bioeconomy and circular economy policies. The Convention on Biological Diversity (CBD) plays a central role, particularly through the Kunming-Montreal Global Biodiversity Framework, which calls for integrating biodiversity into all sectors, including agriculture, forestry, and industry. The United Nations Framework Convention on Climate Change (UNFCCC) supports climate-aligned bioeconomy pathways through national climate commitments that include sustainable land use and carbon sequestration. The Basel Convention on the Control of Transboundary Movements of Hazardous Wastes and Their

Disposal also affects trade in waste-derived bio-based materials, especially where contamination or mixed waste streams are involved.

Trade policies shape the movement of bio-based products and influence the environmental standards that apply across markets. Tariff structures, technical barriers to trade, and sustainability standards can either support or hinder the growth of circular bioeconomy sectors. For example, preferential tariffs for certified bio-based products, or mutual recognition of sustainability certifications, can create incentives for responsible production and consumption. Conversely, the absence of harmonized definitions and sustainability criteria may lead to trade disputes, market fragmentation, or the displacement of environmental harms to jurisdictions with weaker regulations.

Cross-border governance arrangements, such as bilateral agreements, regional trade blocs, and multilateral platforms, offer mechanisms for aligning policies and fostering cooperation. The European Union's Circular Economy Action Plan and Bioeconomy Strategy provide a model of coordinated regional governance, combining regulatory frameworks, investment strategies, and research initiatives. Outside the EU, regional organizations and trade alliances are beginning to explore similar approaches to align environmental standards and facilitate the flow of sustainable bio-based goods.

One challenge is the potential for leakage, where environmental burdens shift from countries with strong regulations to those with more lenient enforcement. To address this, cross-border governance must include provisions for transparency, enforcement, and mutual accountability. Mechanisms such as sustainability-linked trade agreements, environmental side accords, or joint monitoring frameworks can help prevent backsliding and promote a level playing field.

Technology transfer, capacity building, and equitable benefit-sharing are also critical components of international cooperation. Many lower-income countries are rich in biological resources but may lack the infrastructure, governance capacity, or investment required to participate in high-value circular bioeconomy markets. International finance and knowledge-sharing initiatives can support inclusive development, while intellectual property frameworks must be designed to prevent exploitation and ensure fair recognition of traditional knowledge and local innovation.

International conventions, trade policies, and cross-border governance systems must work together to ensure that the growth of the circular bioeconomy enhances ecological integrity, respects social equity, and contributes to global sustainability goals. Coherence, transparency, and collaboration across borders are key to avoiding fragmentation and ensuring that circularity and regeneration extend beyond national boundaries.

Institutional Coordination: Agriculture, Environment, Industry, and Innovation Ministries

Institutional coordination is fundamental to the success of a nature-positive circular bioeconomy. The sectors involved—agriculture, environment, industry, and innovation—often operate under separate mandates, budgets, and policy frameworks. Without alignment, efforts to promote circularity, bio-based innovation, and ecological regeneration may conflict, overlap, or remain fragmented. Effective coordination ensures that policies, investments, and implementation efforts are coherent, mutually reinforcing, and capable of delivering integrated outcomes across economic and ecological systems.

The agriculture ministry typically focuses on food security, rural development, and productivity. Its policies influence land use, biomass availability, and farming practices that directly affect biodiversity, soil health, and emissions. To support circular bioeconomy objectives, this ministry can promote regenerative agriculture, incentivize residue valorization, and support the integration of agroecological principles into national development plans.

The environment ministry is tasked with biodiversity conservation, climate mitigation, pollution control, and natural resource management. It plays a critical role in setting ecological boundaries, enforcing environmental safeguards, and integrating ecosystem restoration into policy frameworks. Collaboration with the agriculture ministry can help align land management with conservation goals, while partnerships with industry can ensure that waste regulation and material standards support circular practices.

The industry ministry oversees manufacturing, resource extraction, infrastructure, and economic competitiveness. It is often the lead body in supporting value-added bio-based production, green jobs, and industrial symbiosis. To contribute to a nature-positive transition, this ministry must integrate environmental criteria into industrial development strategies, support circular product design, and enable cleaner production processes that use renewable and non-toxic inputs.

The innovation or science and technology ministry is central to supporting research, scaling emerging technologies, and building the knowledge base for circular bioeconomy systems. It can help fund interdisciplinary innovation clusters, promote knowledge-sharing platforms, and align national research priorities with circularity and regeneration. Coordination with other ministries ensures that technological development responds to real-world needs and is deployed in a way that maximizes environmental and social impact.

Mechanisms for institutional coordination may include inter-ministerial committees, national circular economy councils, or bioeconomy task forces. These bodies can facilitate dialogue, share data, align funding mechanisms, and monitor progress toward shared targets. Cross-sectoral policy instruments—such as integrated bioeconomy strategies, sustainability frameworks, or land-use plans—also help clarify roles and responsibilities while fostering accountability.

Clear communication channels, shared objectives, and joint performance indicators are necessary for maintaining alignment over time. Coordination should extend to sub-national levels, where regional and local governments play key roles in implementation. Engaging stakeholders from academia, civil society, and the private sector further strengthens institutional alignment by ensuring diverse perspectives and practical insights are reflected in policy and program design.

Institutional coordination across agriculture, environment, industry, and innovation ministries supports systemic thinking and enables more effective use of public resources. It ensures that economic transformation efforts do not undermine ecological integrity or social inclusion, but instead work collectively to support a sustainable, circular, and regenerative bioeconomy.

Pathways for Mainstreaming Nature-Positive Metrics into National Planning

Integrating nature-positive metrics into national planning is essential for aligning economic development with ecological integrity and long-term resilience. While many national strategies acknowledge sustainability goals, they often lack concrete, measurable indicators that reflect ecosystem health, biodiversity outcomes, and regenerative land use. Mainstreaming nature-positive metrics ensures that environmental performance is not treated as a separate agenda but embedded across policy domains, investment frameworks, and planning processes.

One foundational pathway is the adoption of standardized metrics and accounting frameworks that reflect ecological conditions and ecosystem services. These may include indicators such as species richness, habitat connectivity, soil organic carbon, pollination potential, or water retention capacity. Aligning with global frameworks like the System of Environmental-Economic Accounting—Ecosystem Accounting (SEEA-EA) can provide a consistent basis for integrating natural capital into national accounts and policy targets.

A second pathway involves embedding nature-positive metrics into key development strategies and sectoral plans. For example, national agriculture plans can include targets for soil regeneration or landscape-level biodiversity, while industrial policies can track the use of renewable bio-based inputs and closed-loop systems. Climate adaptation and mitigation strategies can incorporate ecosystem-based indicators to assess the co-benefits of land use, forestry, and water management.

Public investment programs and infrastructure projects offer another entry point. Environmental screening criteria can be updated to include nature-positive indicators alongside conventional environmental impact assessments. Performance-based budgeting can allocate funds based on progress toward ecological regeneration goals, ensuring that nature outcomes influence financial decision-making.

National monitoring and reporting systems should be enhanced to collect, analyze, and disseminate data related to nature-positive outcomes. This includes supporting data platforms that integrate satellite monitoring, field data, and citizen science, and that can inform both national assessments and local decision-making. Integration with spatial planning tools allows for visualizing trade-offs and synergies between land uses, guiding more informed policy design.

Cross-sectoral coordination is necessary to ensure that different ministries and agencies apply consistent metrics and share a common understanding of what constitutes nature-positive outcomes. Establishing interagency working groups or task forces focused on ecosystem accounting and biodiversity indicators helps promote coherence and institutional learning.

Engagement with local governments and communities ensures that national indicators are grounded in local realities and responsive to context-specific priorities. This is particularly important for recognizing the contributions of indigenous knowledge and community-based conservation to broader environmental objectives.

Finally, international cooperation and peer learning can help countries refine and apply nature-positive metrics. Participation in global initiatives—such as the Taskforce on Nature-related Financial Disclosures (TNFD), the UN Biodiversity Lab, or regional biodiversity platforms—provides access to technical guidance, comparative tools, and capacity-building support.

By mainstreaming nature-positive metrics into national planning, governments can move beyond aspirational goals toward measurable, accountable progress. This approach supports transparency, aligns with global sustainability commitments, and creates the basis for policies and investments that contribute meaningfully to biodiversity conservation, ecosystem restoration, and a regenerative circular bioeconomy.

Chapter 7. Urban and Regional Integration of Circular Bioeconomy Models

Urban and regional systems are key arenas for implementing nature-positive circular bioeconomy models. Cities are major consumers of biomass-based goods and generators of organic waste, while surrounding regions often supply the biological resources that sustain urban economies. Integrating circular bioeconomy practices at these interconnected scales creates opportunities to close material loops, enhance resource efficiency, and restore ecosystems across urban–rural interfaces.

This chapter explores strategies for embedding circular bioeconomy principles into urban and regional planning, infrastructure, and governance. It examines how material flows—such as food, water, energy, and biomass—can be recirculated through systems like composting, biorefineries, urban farming, and green infrastructure. Special attention is given to city-region food systems, organic waste valorization, and the role of municipalities in supporting circular transitions.

The chapter also highlights regional bioeconomy hubs and industrial symbiosis as models for fostering local collaboration, innovation, and shared infrastructure. It discusses the importance of spatial planning, stakeholder coordination, and data tools to enable circularity at scale.

By focusing on integrated, place-based approaches, this chapter illustrates how cities and regions can become drivers of regenerative development. It shows that aligning circular bioeconomy models with local ecological, economic, and social contexts is essential for building resilient and inclusive systems.

Urban Metabolism and Nature-Positive Circular Resource Loops

Urban metabolism refers to the flow of materials, energy, water, and waste into, within, and out of cities. Understanding these flows is critical for designing circular systems that reduce pressure on natural resources and ecosystems while improving urban resilience and sustainability. In the context of a nature-positive circular bioeconomy, the goal is not only to minimize urban environmental impacts but to actively regenerate natural systems through closed-loop resource use and ecological integration.

Cities are major consumers of biomass and generators of organic waste. Food, wood, textiles, paper, and green waste all pass through urban centers, often in linear pathways that result in waste accumulation, emissions, and the degradation of natural resources. Urban metabolism analysis helps identify where these flows can be redirected, slowed, or closed through circular loops such as reuse, composting, anaerobic digestion, and biobased manufacturing.

A nature-positive approach extends traditional circularity by ensuring that resource loops contribute to ecological regeneration. For example, composted organic waste can be returned to peri-urban farms to restore soil fertility and increase carbon sequestration. Treated wastewater and biosolids from urban sanitation systems can be safely reused in agriculture or green infrastructure projects, improving water retention and nutrient cycling. Such practices reduce the environmental footprint of cities while supporting ecosystem services in surrounding landscapes.

Urban food systems offer significant opportunities for nature-positive circular loops. Surplus food redistribution, home and community composting, and the use of food waste in insect farming or biogas production all reduce waste and create new value streams. These interventions also support local food resilience and reduce the demand for resource-intensive supply chains.

Green and blue infrastructure—such as green roofs, bioswales, urban forests, and wetlands—can be integrated with resource recovery systems to manage stormwater, purify air, and provide habitats. These features can be designed to function as part of the urban metabolic system, absorbing and reusing organic materials, water, and nutrients generated by the city itself.

Digital tools, including urban metabolism modeling and GIS-based planning platforms, enable cities to map material flows and identify circularity opportunities. These tools help planners and policymakers understand the interactions between consumption, waste generation, and ecological impact at different scales, guiding interventions that optimize system performance and regenerative outcomes.

Institutional coordination is key to implementing circular resource loops in urban settings. Waste management authorities, water utilities, urban planners, and environmental agencies must work together to align goals, infrastructure investments, and regulatory frameworks. Local governments can support nature-positive loops by setting procurement criteria for bio-based products, creating incentives for decentralized composting or reuse systems, and integrating circularity into zoning and development policies.

By reconfiguring urban metabolism around circular and regenerative principles, cities can become active contributors to environmental recovery. This approach not only reduces resource extraction and emissions but also enhances biodiversity, ecosystem function, and social well-being within and beyond urban boundaries.

Circular Bioeconomy in City-Region Food Systems and Organic Waste Cycles

City-region food systems represent the interconnected network of food production, distribution, consumption, and waste management within and around urban areas. Integrating circular bioeconomy principles into these systems enables the transition from linear, extractive models to regenerative ones that reduce environmental impact, enhance food security, and create new economic opportunities. Central to this transition is the effective management of organic waste cycles, which form a critical feedback loop between urban consumption and rural production.

Urban areas generate significant volumes of organic waste, including food scraps, green waste, and biomass residues from processing and retail activities. In conventional systems, this material is often landfilled or incinerated, resulting in methane emissions, nutrient loss, and missed opportunities for resource recovery. A circular bioeconomy approach repositions organic waste as a valuable input for new food, energy, and material production processes.

One key strategy is nutrient recovery through composting and anaerobic digestion. Compost produced from separated organic waste can be returned to peri-urban and rural farms to improve soil fertility, structure, and microbial health. Anaerobic digestion yields biogas and digestate, providing renewable energy and a nutrient-rich by-product that can replace synthetic fertilizers. These processes close nutrient loops, reduce greenhouse gas emissions, and support regenerative agriculture.

Food waste prevention is a high-priority intervention that complements resource recovery. Initiatives such as surplus redistribution, food-sharing platforms, and real-time inventory systems in retail and hospitality sectors reduce the volume of edible food lost. Municipal policies, education campaigns, and public procurement standards can support these efforts and align stakeholders across the supply chain.

Circularity in city-region food systems also involves localizing production and shortening supply chains. Urban and peri-urban agriculture—including rooftop farms, community gardens, and vertical growing systems—can reduce transportation emissions, promote seasonal consumption, and recycle organic inputs more easily. These systems benefit from circular inputs such as compost, biochar, or nutrient-enriched irrigation water sourced from urban biowaste treatment.

Organic waste cycles can be extended beyond energy and compost to support material innovation. Startups and social enterprises are transforming food and agricultural residues into bioplastics, packaging, textiles, and construction materials. Banana peels, coffee grounds, and mushroom mycelium are just a few of the bio-based inputs used to create circular products with reduced environmental footprints.

Governance and infrastructure are crucial enablers. Cities must invest in decentralized waste collection systems, separation at source, and organic waste treatment facilities that serve both urban and rural communities. Clear standards, consistent labeling, and supportive regulation ensure that organic waste streams are safe and fit for circular use. Integration with rural development strategies and regional planning supports a coordinated approach across city-region boundaries.

Engaging communities and businesses in co-designing food and waste cycles strengthens social buy-in and fosters innovation. Education, incentives, and recognition programs can build a culture of circularity and support behavioral change across all stages of the food system.

By embedding circular bioeconomy principles into city-region food systems and organic waste cycles, cities can improve resilience, reduce pressure on ecosystems, and generate regenerative value for both urban and rural populations. This approach enhances food system sustainability while contributing to broader climate and biodiversity goals.

Integrating Green Infrastructure with Bio-Waste Valorization

Integrating green infrastructure with bio-waste valorization creates multifunctional urban systems that enhance ecosystem services, reduce waste, and support the principles of a nature-positive circular bioeconomy. This approach links the design and management of urban green spaces—such as parks, green roofs, rain gardens, and urban forests—with the processing and reuse of organic waste streams, creating feedback loops that benefit both urban resilience and ecological regeneration.

Green infrastructure plays a critical role in managing water, improving air quality, regulating temperature, and providing habitat in densely built environments. When designed with circularity in mind, it can also become a productive sink for nutrients and organic matter recovered from urban biowaste. Compost, digestate, and biochar derived from food waste, garden trimmings, and sewage sludge can be applied to soils in green infrastructure projects, improving soil health, enhancing carbon sequestration, and supporting plant growth.

One application is the use of compost in soil amendment for street trees, green belts, and community gardens. This supports plant health, reduces the need for synthetic fertilizers, and improves stormwater infiltration. Similarly, digestate from anaerobic digestion processes can be used to irrigate and fertilize green spaces, provided that it meets safety and contamination standards.

Biochar produced from woody waste or agricultural residues can be incorporated into green infrastructure to improve soil structure, increase water retention, and reduce nutrient leaching. Its long-term carbon storage potential also contributes to climate mitigation efforts. When used in bioswales or rain gardens, biochar can enhance pollutant filtration and support vegetation adapted to fluctuating water levels.

Green roofs and living walls present additional opportunities for integrating bio-waste valorization. Lightweight compost or biochar-based growing media can support rooftop vegetation while recycling organic matter generated within the city. This not only diverts waste from landfill but also increases building insulation, reduces urban heat island effects, and provides habitat for pollinators.

Integration can also occur at the infrastructure level. Urban composting and anaerobic digestion facilities can be co-located with parks, nurseries, or landscaping depots to create local material loops. The proximity of green spaces to organic waste processing sites reduces transportation needs and encourages community involvement in waste separation and resource recovery.

Policy and planning mechanisms are needed to support integration. Urban development regulations can require green infrastructure in new projects and promote the use of recycled organic inputs in landscaping and public works. Municipal procurement policies can prioritize soil products and fertilizers derived from locally processed biowaste, supporting local circular economies.

Education and community engagement are important for building public support and participation. Residents, schools, and businesses can be involved in composting initiatives and greening efforts, reinforcing the connection between waste reduction and environmental enhancement.

Integrating green infrastructure with bio-waste valorization aligns urban development with ecological cycles. It supports circular flows of nutrients and organic matter, reduces reliance on external inputs, and enhances the functionality and resilience of urban ecosystems. This holistic approach contributes to more livable, regenerative cities that actively support biodiversity, climate goals, and sustainable resource use.

Biocities and Regenerative Urban Design Principles

Biocities represent an emerging model of urban development that integrates circular economy practices with ecological restoration, social well-being, and systems thinking. They go beyond sustainability by aiming to regenerate natural systems, restore ecosystem functions, and create cities that are net contributors to biodiversity, climate resilience, and resource renewal. Central to the biocity concept is the application of regenerative urban design principles that embed nature and circularity into the very fabric of urban planning and development.

Regenerative urban design focuses on creating built environments that enhance, rather than deplete, the ecological systems in which they are embedded. This requires cities to operate like living systems, with closed-loop resource flows, multifunctional infrastructure, and active support for ecosystem services such as carbon sequestration, water purification, pollination, and climate regulation.

One of the key principles is designing with natural systems, which involves aligning city layouts, land use, and infrastructure with the contours of local watersheds, soil conditions, and biodiversity corridors. Green corridors, urban wetlands, and restored riverbanks are used to reconnect fragmented habitats, support native species, and manage stormwater naturally.

Another principle is material circularity, where the construction, renovation, and operation of buildings prioritize renewable, bio-based, and recycled materials. Buildings are designed for disassembly, reuse, and adaptive reuse, reducing waste and enabling materials to remain in use for as long as possible. Organic waste from urban areas is processed and returned to support soil health, urban farming, and landscape regeneration.

Energy and water systems in biocities are decentralized and renewable. Rainwater harvesting, greywater recycling, and wastewater treatment are integrated into buildings and neighborhoods. Renewable energy sources, such as solar and bioenergy from organic waste, are embedded into local grids, reducing reliance on centralized, fossil-fuel-based infrastructure.

Public spaces are reimagined as multifunctional landscapes that serve ecological, social, and economic functions. Parks, green roofs, urban forests, and community gardens provide habitat, food production, and recreation, while also improving air quality and reducing heat stress. These spaces are co-designed with communities to reflect local culture and promote inclusivity.

Mobility systems in regenerative cities emphasize walkability, cycling, and public transport, reducing emissions and land-use pressure. Streetscapes are designed to support biodiversity through permeable surfaces, native vegetation, and green buffers.

Governance plays a critical role in enabling biocities. Integrated planning frameworks, participatory design processes, and long-term investment in nature-based infrastructure are necessary to scale regenerative practices. Cross-sector collaboration between urban planners, architects, ecologists, engineers, and communities ensures that diverse knowledge systems inform design and implementation.

Data-driven decision-making supports performance monitoring and continuous improvement. Metrics include biodiversity indicators, material and energy flows, soil and water quality, and social inclusion outcomes. These data inform urban planning and guide adaptive management over time.

Biocities and regenerative urban design principles reflect a shift from minimizing harm to actively restoring ecological and social systems. They demonstrate how urban areas can become engines of regeneration, contributing positively to the health of the planet and the well-being of current and future generations.

Role of Municipalities in Closing Loops and Restoring Biodiversity

Municipalities play a central role in advancing a nature-positive circular bioeconomy by acting as facilitators, regulators, and implementers of local strategies that close resource loops and restore biodiversity. Their proximity to citizens, infrastructure, and waste streams enables them to design context-specific solutions, integrate ecological thinking into urban systems, and build strong partnerships across sectors.

One of the primary responsibilities of municipalities is waste and resource management. Local governments can establish systems for source separation, collection, and treatment of organic waste, enabling its transformation into compost, biogas, or soil amendments. These outputs can be reintegrated into local food systems, green infrastructure, or peri-urban farms, closing nutrient and carbon loops within city boundaries. Municipalities can also develop decentralized waste processing facilities, such as community composting hubs or small-scale anaerobic digesters, to reduce transportation emissions and engage communities in circular practices.

Land use planning and zoning policies are powerful tools that municipalities can use to protect and restore biodiversity. By designating ecological corridors, preserving urban forests, limiting impervious surfaces, and encouraging native landscaping, municipalities can increase habitat availability and connectivity. Planning instruments can also mandate the inclusion of green infrastructure in new developments and promote the restoration of degraded sites through rewilding, wetland creation, or soil regeneration.

Urban greening initiatives provide opportunities to integrate biodiversity into everyday public spaces. Tree planting programs, pollinator corridors, and biodiversity-friendly park designs enhance ecological function while improving quality of life. Municipalities can also promote biodiversity on public lands by adopting ecological maintenance practices, avoiding chemical use, and incorporating habitat features such as nesting sites and native plantings.

Procurement policies offer another avenue for municipalities to influence supply chains and close material loops. By prioritizing circular, bio-based, and locally produced goods in public tenders, municipalities can stimulate demand for sustainable materials and reduce waste. Contracts for catering, construction, and maintenance services can include requirements for compostable packaging, recycled content, or low-impact materials.

Municipalities can also support local businesses, social enterprises, and cooperatives engaged in bio-circular activities. This includes providing access to land, funding pilot projects, simplifying permitting processes, or offering technical assistance for startups in composting, urban farming, or bio-based innovation. Partnerships with universities, civil society, and the private sector can foster knowledge sharing and co-create solutions adapted to local needs.

Education and community engagement are essential to build public understanding of biodiversity and circular practices. Municipalities can run awareness campaigns, support citizen science, and involve residents in urban greening, restoration projects, or food waste reduction programs. Schools, libraries, and community centers can serve as hubs for environmental learning and participation.

To be effective, municipal efforts must be embedded in broader governance frameworks. Coordination with regional and national governments ensures alignment with biodiversity strategies, climate action plans, and circular economy policies. Access to funding, technical expertise, and monitoring tools enhances the capacity of municipalities to act.

By leveraging their planning authority, operational responsibilities, and community connections, municipalities are uniquely positioned to implement integrated solutions that restore nature and build circular systems. Their actions at the local level are essential for realizing global biodiversity and sustainability goals.

Regional Bioeconomy Hubs and Industrial Symbiosis

Regional bioeconomy hubs and industrial symbiosis are strategic frameworks that enable collaboration, efficiency, and value creation across sectors and supply chains within a defined geographic area. These models are essential for scaling the circular bioeconomy while ensuring that economic activity supports ecological regeneration and community resilience.

A regional bioeconomy hub is typically a cluster of businesses, research institutions, infrastructure, and public agencies focused on the production, processing, and valorization of biological resources. These hubs are designed to harness local biomass streams—such as agricultural residues, forestry by-products, and organic waste—and convert them into high-value products including bio-based materials, renewable energy, biochemicals, and soil amendments. By concentrating activities and actors in a region, hubs can achieve economies of scale, reduce logistical costs, and foster innovation through knowledge exchange.

The effectiveness of these hubs depends on coordinated planning and investment. Local feedstock availability, transportation networks, and market demand shape the viability of a hub, while public policy can support its development through land-use planning, financial incentives, and regulatory alignment. Regional bioeconomy hubs often involve partnerships between municipalities, private sector firms, universities, and community organizations to co-develop projects and share infrastructure.

Industrial symbiosis within these hubs further enhances circularity and resource efficiency. This approach involves the exchange of materials, energy, water, and by-products between co-located industries. For example, a biogas facility might supply heat to a greenhouse, which in turn provides organic waste to the digester. A sawmill could supply wood residues to a biocomposite manufacturer, whose scrap could be used for bioenergy or compost production. These exchanges reduce waste, lower operational costs, and support diversified revenue streams.

Digital platforms and mapping tools can facilitate industrial symbiosis by identifying potential material flows, matching businesses with complementary needs, and optimizing supply logistics. Collaborative governance structures, such as regional circular economy networks or innovation councils, help coordinate actors, address regulatory barriers, and build trust among participants.

In addition to environmental and economic benefits, regional hubs and symbiosis models can contribute to social objectives. They support job creation in rural and peri-urban areas, enable skills development in emerging sectors, and foster local ownership of the bioeconomy transition. Community participation and equitable benefit-sharing are important to ensure that regional development aligns with inclusive sustainability goals.

These models also strengthen resilience by reducing dependence on global supply chains and external inputs. Localizing biomass processing and product manufacturing increases adaptability to resource shocks, market volatility, and environmental disruptions.

To scale and replicate regional bioeconomy hubs and industrial symbiosis, enabling conditions must include consistent policy support, access to finance, robust infrastructure, and long-term planning. Integration with regional climate and biodiversity strategies ensures that growth is not only circular but regenerative.

Together, regional bioeconomy hubs and industrial symbiosis provide a practical and systemic approach to building place-based circular economies that restore ecosystems, reduce waste, and support thriving local economies.

Chapter 8. Nature-Positive Metrics, Indicators, and Monitoring Frameworks

Measuring progress in a nature-positive circular bioeconomy requires robust metrics, indicators, and monitoring frameworks that capture environmental regeneration, material circularity, and biodiversity outcomes. Traditional efficiency metrics are not sufficient for assessing whether systems are operating within planetary boundaries or contributing to ecological restoration. A more integrated approach is needed—one that links resource flows with ecosystem health and long-term resilience.

This chapter introduces the tools and frameworks used to assess circularity and nature-positive performance. It explores indicators such as material circularity rates, ecosystem condition, species richness, functional diversity, and nutrient cycling. It also discusses the role of decoupling indicators, lifecycle assessment, and natural capital accounting in evaluating both the impacts and benefits of circular bioeconomy systems.

Attention is given to science-based targets and how they can be translated into actionable goals for businesses, governments, and communities. The chapter examines the importance of open-access platforms, data transparency, and participatory monitoring in supporting accountability and adaptive management.

By presenting practical guidance on how to define, track, and communicate progress, this chapter underscores the importance of evidence-based approaches to policy, investment, and planning. It shows how metrics can align circular bioeconomy efforts with broader environmental objectives and reinforce a shared commitment to regeneration.

Frameworks for Assessing Circularity, Regeneration, and Biodiversity Impact

Measuring progress in a nature-positive circular bioeconomy requires integrated assessment frameworks that capture material efficiency, ecological regeneration, and biodiversity outcomes. Traditional metrics focused solely on resource use or emissions reduction are insufficient for evaluating whether systems are truly circular and regenerative. A more comprehensive approach links circularity with positive ecological performance, enabling decision-makers to design, implement, and monitor actions that contribute to long-term sustainability.

Circularity assessment frameworks typically focus on material and energy flows, product life cycles, and system efficiency. Tools such as Material Flow Analysis (MFA) and Life Cycle Assessment (LCA) quantify resource inputs, outputs, and impacts across the supply chain. Indicators include material circularity rate, product lifespan, recycling efficiency, and renewable content. These frameworks are useful for identifying hotspots, improving resource productivity, and designing closed-loop systems.

To assess regenerative potential, frameworks must go beyond harm reduction and measure contributions to ecosystem recovery and resilience. Regenerative indicators may include improvements in soil organic carbon, water infiltration, native vegetation cover, or ecological function. Monitoring these outcomes often requires site-specific data and time-series analysis, making them more complex than standard circularity assessments. Nevertheless, they are critical for understanding whether bio-based systems support the recovery of degraded land and ecosystems.

Biodiversity impact assessment tools are designed to evaluate how economic activities affect species, habitats, and ecosystem integrity. Metrics may include species richness, habitat connectivity, ecosystem condition, or functional diversity. The Biodiversity Intactness Index (BII), Mean Species Abundance (MSA), and habitat quality scores are commonly used at regional and project levels. These tools help ensure that circular economy activities, including biomass sourcing and waste valorization, do not compromise biodiversity and instead contribute to its restoration.

Several integrated frameworks are emerging to combine these dimensions:

- The Natural Capital Protocol provides guidance for assessing business impacts and dependencies on nature, including both resource use and ecological condition.
- The European Commission's Circular Economy Monitoring Framework includes indicators on production, consumption, waste management, and secondary raw materials, with some links to environmental impacts.
- The Taskforce on Nature-related Financial Disclosures (TNFD) framework supports organizations in identifying and managing nature-related risks and opportunities, promoting the use of biodiversity metrics in decision-making.
- The Regenerative Agriculture Frameworks developed by NGOs and certification bodies include biodiversity and ecosystem health metrics alongside soil and water indicators.

To operationalize these frameworks, reliable data and context-specific baselines are essential. Geospatial tools, remote sensing, and sensor technologies can support large-scale monitoring, while stakeholder engagement helps ensure that assessments reflect local realities and priorities.

Effective assessment frameworks must be transparent, adaptable, and aligned with policy and investment goals. They should support continuous improvement, enable cross-comparison, and inform policy design, certification, and corporate reporting.

By applying integrated frameworks that assess circularity, regeneration, and biodiversity impact together, stakeholders can better understand trade-offs, identify synergies, and guide systems toward outcomes that are not just less harmful but actively restorative.

Absolute Versus Relative Decoupling Indicators

Decoupling indicators are used to evaluate whether economic growth is becoming less dependent on environmental pressure. In the context of a nature-positive circular bioeconomy, these indicators help assess the extent to which resource use, emissions, or biodiversity impacts are being reduced while maintaining or increasing economic activity. Understanding the difference between absolute and relative decoupling is essential for interpreting sustainability performance and setting meaningful targets.

Relative decoupling occurs when environmental impacts grow at a slower rate than economic output. For example, if a country's GDP increases by 4 percent while its greenhouse gas emissions rise by 1 percent, there is a relative decoupling of emissions from economic growth. While this shows improved efficiency, it still implies an overall increase in environmental pressure, which may be incompatible with planetary boundaries if sustained over time.

Absolute decoupling, by contrast, occurs when environmental impacts decline in absolute terms while the economy continues to grow. Using the same example, if GDP grows by 4 percent but emissions fall by 2 percent, absolute decoupling has occurred. This is considered a more robust indicator of progress toward sustainability, as it signals that economic growth is not only more efficient but is also reducing its environmental footprint in real terms.

In a circular bioeconomy, decoupling indicators can be applied to various domains:

- **Material use**: Absolute decoupling would mean a reduction in the total amount of biomass or raw materials extracted despite economic growth, while relative decoupling would reflect a slower rate of material input per unit of GDP.
- **Waste generation**: Relative decoupling might indicate that waste intensity per economic output is declining, while absolute decoupling would require a total reduction in waste volumes.

- **Land use and biodiversity loss**: Absolute decoupling would require shrinking the land footprint or reducing biodiversity impacts even as bio-based production expands, whereas relative decoupling would show a lower rate of ecosystem disruption per unit of production.

Indicators commonly used to measure decoupling include material footprint per capita, greenhouse gas emissions per GDP, and land-use change relative to agricultural output. These metrics can be tracked over time to monitor trends and evaluate policy effectiveness.

While relative decoupling can be a sign of progress, it may not be sufficient in regions where ecological limits have already been exceeded. Absolute decoupling is more aligned with the goals of ecological regeneration and long-term planetary stability. However, achieving absolute decoupling is complex and often requires transformative changes in production systems, consumption patterns, and economic structures.

To support accurate measurement, decoupling indicators should be accompanied by disaggregated data, system boundaries, and contextual benchmarks. This ensures that improvements are not the result of shifting impacts to other regions or sectors.

Absolute decoupling serves as a key benchmark for aligning economic activity with environmental regeneration in a truly nature-positive circular bioeconomy.

Nature-Positive Indicators: Ecosystem Condition, Species Richness, Functional Diversity

Nature-positive indicators are essential tools for measuring whether economic and policy actions contribute to the recovery, maintenance, and enhancement of natural systems. Unlike conventional environmental metrics that focus on harm reduction or efficiency, nature-positive indicators aim to evaluate net positive outcomes for biodiversity and ecosystem function. In a circular bioeconomy context, they help ensure that biomass use, land management, and material flows actively support ecological regeneration.

Three key indicators commonly used to assess nature-positive outcomes are ecosystem condition, species richness, and functional diversity. Each provides a distinct lens on ecosystem health and resilience.

- Ecosystem condition refers to the physical, biological, and chemical state of an ecosystem relative to its natural or reference condition. It encompasses indicators such as vegetation cover, soil structure, hydrological integrity, and the presence of native species. Improvements in ecosystem condition reflect enhanced capacity to provide ecosystem services like carbon storage, water filtration, and erosion control. In practical terms, this indicator can be measured through habitat quality assessments, remote sensing data, or site-level ecological surveys.
- Species richness measures the number of different species present in a given area. It is a simple but widely used indicator of biodiversity. High species richness generally reflects a stable and diverse ecosystem, while declines may indicate environmental degradation or habitat fragmentation. Monitoring species richness helps identify areas of ecological importance, assess the impact of land-use change, and guide habitat restoration efforts in bioeconomy supply chains.
- Functional diversity captures the range of biological traits within a community that influence how ecosystems function and respond to change. These traits may include differences in nutrient uptake, reproduction, growth rate, or habitat preference. Functional diversity is a strong predictor of ecosystem resilience, as diverse trait combinations allow ecosystems to maintain services under stress. Measuring this indicator often requires field data and ecological expertise, but it provides deeper insight into ecosystem dynamics than species counts alone.

Nature-positive metrics should be applied at appropriate spatial and temporal scales, with baselines established to detect change over time. They can be used in combination with remote sensing technologies, citizen science platforms, and biodiversity monitoring networks. Integrating them into environmental impact assessments, natural capital accounting, and land-use planning frameworks helps ensure that decisions are aligned with regeneration goals.

These indicators are also useful for informing sustainability certifications, supply chain traceability systems, and nature-related disclosures by businesses and governments. By linking bioeconomy activities with measurable ecological outcomes, nature-positive indicators provide a foundation for evidence-based decision-making and accountability in transitioning toward truly regenerative systems.

Material Circularity Indicators for Bio-Based Systems

Material circularity indicators are critical for evaluating how effectively bio-based systems retain material value, minimize waste, and enable closed-loop resource flows. While many general circularity metrics apply across sectors, bio-based systems require specific attention to biological cycles, regenerative potential, and compatibility with end-of-life pathways such as composting, anaerobic digestion, or soil return. These indicators help assess whether bio-based products and processes contribute to a circular and nature-positive economy.

Key material circularity indicators for bio-based systems include:

• **Biogenic content share**

Measures the proportion of a product or material derived from renewable biological sources. A higher biogenic content indicates reduced dependence on fossil-based inputs. This indicator is relevant for assessing the sustainability of bioplastics, bio-based textiles, and packaging materials.

• Bio-based feedstock circularity rate

Captures the share of bio-based inputs sourced from secondary or recovered biomass, such as agricultural residues, food waste, or forestry by-products. It distinguishes between primary biomass extraction and circular feedstock recovery, helping to evaluate pressure on land and ecosystems.

• Material retention rate

Indicates the proportion of material that remains in use through reuse, refurbishment, or recycling before final disposal. For bio-based systems, this may include composting, anaerobic digestion, or conversion into biochar, rather than landfill or incineration.

• Compostability and biodegradability compliance

Tracks whether bio-based products meet standards for industrial or home composting, or biodegradation under specific conditions. This helps determine compatibility with organic recovery streams and supports claims of environmental safety at end-of-life.

• Mass recovery efficiency

Measures the total mass of material recovered from bio-based products as a percentage of the original input. This includes outputs from biowaste valorization processes such as digestate, compost, or extracted nutrients.

• Product lifespan extension

Evaluates the ability of bio-based products to be reused, repaired, or remanufactured before biological degradation. Durable applications (e.g. construction materials, furniture) contribute more to circularity than single-use disposable items.

• **End-of-life routing accuracy**

Reflects the share of bio-based products correctly routed to their intended recovery pathway (e.g. composting facilities vs. mixed waste bins). This indicator depends on waste separation systems, labelling clarity, and user behavior.

• **Displacement potential of virgin materials**

Assesses how effectively circular bio-based materials substitute for new, virgin materials—whether fossil-based or biogenic. This can be quantified through lifecycle analysis comparing environmental impacts.

To ensure meaningful results, these indicators should be applied with defined system boundaries, timeframes, and assumptions about degradation, contamination, or collection infrastructure. When combined, they provide a comprehensive view of how well bio-based systems are performing in terms of circularity, material efficiency, and alignment with regenerative outcomes.

Applying material circularity indicators to bio-based systems supports better product design, supply chain optimization, and policy evaluation. It also enables tracking of progress toward circular economy goals while ensuring that biological materials cycle safely, efficiently, and in harmony with ecological systems.

Data Transparency and Open-Access Platforms

Data transparency and open-access platforms are foundational to scaling a nature-positive circular bioeconomy. They enable evidence-based decision-making, foster accountability, and support collaboration among governments, businesses, researchers, and communities. Open access to accurate, timely, and standardized data helps track material flows, environmental impacts, and biodiversity outcomes, while also lowering barriers to innovation and policy alignment.

In the context of circular bio-based systems, data transparency covers multiple dimensions, including feedstock availability, land use, environmental performance, product lifecycle impacts, and biodiversity indicators. Transparent data allows stakeholders to identify inefficiencies, evaluate trade-offs, and optimize the design and operation of circular systems.

Open-access platforms play a central role by hosting, organizing, and disseminating this data in formats that are publicly available and user-friendly. These platforms often aggregate data from multiple sources—government databases, scientific research, satellite monitoring, sensor networks, and citizen science initiatives. Key functions of open-access platforms include:

- Providing spatial data on biomass sources, ecosystem condition, and biodiversity hotspots to inform sustainable land-use planning and bioeconomy development.
- Hosting lifecycle inventory databases for bio-based materials, allowing companies and researchers to assess product impacts and compare alternatives.
- Offering dashboards and visualization tools that track progress on circularity indicators, material flows, emissions reduction, or resource recovery across sectors and regions.
- Enabling traceability of bio-based products through digital tools such as QR codes, blockchain integration, and product passports, which record sourcing, processing, and end-of-life handling.
- Facilitating peer learning and benchmarking by allowing users to explore case studies, performance metrics, and policy models from other jurisdictions or industries.

Data transparency also supports the credibility of sustainability claims. Companies, particularly in the bioeconomy, are increasingly expected to disclose data on raw material sourcing, environmental impacts, and circular practices. Open-access platforms provide a means to publish this information in a standardized way, enabling comparison and independent verification.

Governments can use open platforms to improve regulatory oversight, design more effective incentives, and align national reporting with international frameworks such as the Sustainable Development Goals, the Kunming-Montreal Global Biodiversity Framework, or climate commitments under the Paris Agreement.

Ensuring data quality, interoperability, and accessibility is critical. This includes adopting common standards for data collection and reporting, ensuring metadata is available, and designing platforms that are inclusive and usable across languages and literacy levels.

Privacy and data governance must also be addressed, particularly when data involves sensitive environmental assets, land tenure, or indigenous knowledge. Transparent governance models and stakeholder participation in platform development help maintain trust and ensure relevance.

By advancing data transparency and supporting open-access platforms, stakeholders can collectively drive more informed, inclusive, and adaptive transitions toward circular and regenerative systems. These platforms empower users to engage in circular economy practices, monitor outcomes, and scale innovations that restore ecosystems and optimize resource use.

Science-Based Targets for Circular Bioeconomy Systems

Science-based targets provide measurable, time-bound goals grounded in ecological thresholds and planetary boundaries. In the context of circular bioeconomy systems, these targets guide decision-makers in aligning material flows, land use, and production practices with climate stability, biodiversity conservation, and resource sustainability. Unlike generic efficiency improvements or voluntary sustainability goals, science-based targets ensure that bioeconomy activities operate within safe and just environmental limits.

Science-based targets for circular bioeconomy systems typically focus on the following domains:

• **Climate mitigation**

Targets are set to reduce greenhouse gas emissions in line with the 1.5°C pathway. This includes emissions from land use, biomass processing, energy consumption, and transportation. Bioeconomy actors can use lifecycle analysis to set emission reduction goals per product or process and transition to renewable inputs, low-carbon technologies, and carbon sequestration practices such as agroforestry or biochar application.

• **Land use and ecosystem integrity**

Targets aim to prevent deforestation, maintain natural habitats, and promote land restoration. Science-based thresholds include halting net conversion of natural ecosystems and ensuring that biomass production supports ecosystem services and biodiversity. This involves spatial planning to protect high conservation value areas and adopting regenerative land management practices.

• **Material circularity**

Targets relate to maintaining materials in use at their highest value, minimizing waste, and reducing the extraction of virgin resources. Metrics include material circularity rate, bio-based feedstock recovery rate, and product reuse or recycling rates. Science-based benchmarks can be drawn from sectoral best practices or modeled scenarios that align with resource decoupling goals.

• Nutrient cycling and pollution reduction

Targets focus on reducing nutrient loss (especially nitrogen and phosphorus) to air and water systems. These are based on safe operating thresholds for eutrophication and soil health. Circular bioeconomy systems set goals for nutrient recovery through composting, anaerobic digestion, or wastewater reuse, aiming to close nutrient loops and eliminate synthetic fertilizer overuse.

• Biodiversity protection

Targets support species and habitat conservation, aligning with frameworks such as the Kunming-Montreal Global Biodiversity Framework. Indicators may include habitat restoration targets, species richness benchmarks, or reduced pressure on threatened species due to sustainable sourcing practices. Businesses can set site- or value-chain-level goals using biodiversity risk and dependency assessments.

• Water stewardship

Targets are set for reducing water withdrawals in water-stressed regions and improving water quality. Bioeconomy actors can apply science-based thresholds by watershed, using tools like water risk assessments and regional water availability data to guide operations and product design.

Developing and implementing science-based targets in the circular bioeconomy requires cross-sector collaboration, robust data, and credible methodologies. Organizations such as the Science Based Targets initiative (SBTi), the Stockholm Resilience Centre, and the Ellen MacArthur Foundation are advancing frameworks and tools to support target-setting for circularity, regeneration, and biodiversity.

Monitoring progress involves selecting appropriate indicators, establishing baselines, and reporting performance transparently.

Integrating targets into procurement, investment, and operational decision-making ensures that they influence real-world outcomes.

Science-based targets help ensure that circular bioeconomy systems contribute not just to resource efficiency or economic development, but to the stability of Earth's life-support systems. They provide a critical reference point for aligning business models, policies, and innovations with the ecological realities of a finite planet.

Chapter 9. Behavioural Change, Cultural Shifts, and Participatory Action

The success of a nature-positive circular bioeconomy depends not only on technology, policy, and finance but also on deep cultural and behavioural transformation. Shifting toward regenerative systems requires rethinking how people produce, consume, relate to nature, and engage with one another. Behavioural change, cultural narratives, and participatory action are essential drivers of this systemic transition.

This chapter explores how education, communication, and social innovation can support the development of circular mindsets and regenerative values. It examines the role of public awareness, community engagement, and citizen science in shaping demand, promoting stewardship, and strengthening accountability. Cultural narratives that emphasize interdependence, care, and ecological restoration are highlighted as powerful tools for reimagining prosperity and redefining success.

The chapter also discusses the importance of inclusive participation—ensuring that individuals, communities, and historically underrepresented groups have a voice in shaping bioeconomy strategies and benefit from the transition. It covers initiatives such as public procurement, local co-design processes, and social enterprise models that bridge cultural, economic, and environmental goals.

By focusing on the human dimension of change, this chapter underscores that the circular bioeconomy is not only a technical shift, but a cultural and collective journey—grounded in shared responsibility, agency, and the regeneration of both ecosystems and communities.

Rethinking Consumption and Production in a Nature-Positive Economy

Transitioning to a nature-positive economy requires a fundamental rethinking of how goods and services are produced and consumed. Current systems are largely linear and extractive—built on the assumption of infinite resource availability and externalized environmental costs. In contrast, a nature-positive economy seeks to decouple well-being and prosperity from material throughput by designing systems that regenerate ecosystems, preserve biodiversity, and operate within planetary boundaries.

Rethinking production starts with redesigning products and services to minimize resource extraction and maximize circularity. This involves shifting from high-volume, disposable models to regenerative, modular, and service-oriented systems. Producers are encouraged to use renewable, bio-based, and recycled materials sourced responsibly and managed in ways that restore soil health, water quality, and habitat integrity.

Business models are evolving from ownership to access and performance-based services. Examples include leasing, product-as-a-service, and sharing platforms that extend product lifespans and reduce the need for virgin material inputs. In the bioeconomy, this may include systems that deliver nutrients, energy, or packaging functions without producing excess waste or pollution.

On the consumption side, behavioral change and demand-side strategies are essential. Consumers play a key role in shaping market dynamics, but must be supported through accessible, affordable, and attractive circular options. Awareness campaigns, eco-labels, digital tools, and repair or reuse services can help shift preferences toward low-impact, regenerative alternatives.

Public procurement is a powerful lever for rethinking both production and consumption. By prioritizing bio-based, compostable, or reusable products, governments can stimulate demand for sustainable innovation and establish new market norms. Education systems can also contribute by embedding circular and ecological thinking into curricula, fostering a culture of care for natural systems.

Policy alignment is critical. Regulatory frameworks need to phase out harmful substances, incentivize regenerative design, and internalize environmental costs. Taxes and subsidies should be structured to reward circular practices and penalize extractive or polluting ones. Extended producer responsibility, product take-back schemes, and material labeling can facilitate closed-loop systems and inform consumer choices.

Digital technologies support this transition by increasing transparency, traceability, and participation. Platforms that connect producers, users, and recyclers can facilitate material recovery, remanufacturing, and peer-to-peer exchanges. Data-driven tools help map resource flows and identify opportunities for intervention and system optimization.

Equity and inclusion are central considerations. Rethinking consumption and production must also address access, affordability, and social innovation. Circular and regenerative practices should create livelihoods, reduce dependency on harmful industries, and support communities—especially in the informal sector or rural bioeconomy regions.

Ultimately, rethinking consumption and production in a nature-positive economy means moving beyond efficiency toward sufficiency and regeneration. It shifts the goal from minimizing harm to creating net-positive outcomes for ecosystems, people, and the economy. This transformation requires not only new technologies and policies, but new values and cultural narratives that place nature at the core of economic systems.

Social Innovation, Citizen Science, and Community Stewardship

Social innovation, citizen science, and community stewardship are key enablers of a nature-positive circular bioeconomy. They support the co-creation of solutions, democratize knowledge, and strengthen the social foundations of ecological regeneration. These approaches empower individuals and communities to actively participate in reshaping local systems of production, consumption, and environmental governance.

Social innovation refers to new practices, models, or collaborations that address social and ecological challenges in ways that are inclusive, participatory, and often grassroots-driven. In the bioeconomy, this might include cooperative composting initiatives, local food-sharing networks, repair cafés, or community-based biowaste valorization schemes. These models prioritize social equity, cultural relevance, and adaptability over top-down technological fixes.

Citizen science involves public participation in the generation of scientific knowledge. Individuals collect data, monitor environmental changes, or contribute to biodiversity assessments using standardized methods. In the context of a nature-positive economy, citizen science supports ecosystem monitoring, tracks circularity outcomes (such as food waste or material recovery), and fills data gaps at local levels. It also builds ecological literacy and strengthens public engagement with environmental issues.

Community stewardship refers to the collective responsibility and care for shared natural resources, including land, water, forests, and biodiversity. Stewardship can take the form of community-managed forests, watershed protection groups, or urban greening projects led by residents. These initiatives ensure that local knowledge, needs, and values shape how resources are used, restored, and maintained over time.

Together, these approaches enhance resilience by rooting solutions in place-based knowledge and social capital. They create trust, foster collaboration, and increase the legitimacy of sustainability policies and projects. Social innovation can also bridge the gap between formal institutions and informal economies, recognizing the role of diverse actors—including youth, elders, and marginalized communities—in the transition to circular and regenerative systems.

Governments and institutions can support these efforts through enabling policies, funding mechanisms, capacity-building, and recognition schemes. Open-access data platforms, citizen monitoring apps, and participatory governance tools help integrate community inputs into formal decision-making. Educational programs, local workshops, and civic labs further support engagement and skills development.

These community-driven efforts are not a substitute for systemic change, but a vital complement. They provide the local momentum and social infrastructure needed to implement and sustain circular bioeconomy strategies. By embedding care, equity, and agency into environmental action, social innovation, citizen science, and stewardship strengthen the cultural and democratic foundations of a nature-positive future.

Cultural Narratives Around Regeneration and Bio-Based Transitions

Cultural narratives shape how societies understand their relationship with nature, technology, and the economy. In the context of a nature-positive circular bioeconomy, cultural narratives play a powerful role in influencing values, behaviors, and public support for regenerative and bio-based transitions. They help frame what is seen as desirable, possible, and necessary, guiding collective imagination and action.

The dominant narrative of industrial modernity has often centered on progress through extraction, consumption, and linear growth. Nature is framed as a resource to be used, and success is measured by material throughput and economic expansion. This narrative underpins many current systems of production and consumption and contributes to environmental degradation and biodiversity loss.

In contrast, regenerative and bio-based narratives emphasize interdependence, renewal, and living within ecological limits. They present humans not as separate from nature, but as participants in natural cycles. Regeneration becomes a core value—one that moves beyond sustainability's goal of minimizing harm to actively improving ecological and social systems.

Key themes in regenerative narratives include:

- **Nature as a partner**: Instead of viewing ecosystems as passive providers of resources, this narrative presents nature as an active collaborator. Biomimicry, agroecology, and ecosystem restoration embody this relationship, where design and management are inspired by natural processes.
- **Circularity as tradition and innovation**: Many Indigenous and local knowledge systems have long embraced circular principles—reusing, repairing, and respecting cycles of life and death. These traditions are increasingly being revalued alongside technological innovation to build culturally grounded and forward-looking solutions.
- **Care and stewardship**: Regenerative narratives center around caring for land, community, and future generations. They promote a sense of responsibility and belonging, where economic activity is shaped by values of restoration, reciprocity, and place-based identity.
- **Redefining prosperity**: A shift from quantity to quality— where well-being is not defined by consumption but by health, connection, creativity, and ecological balance. This reframing supports sufficiency-based lifestyles and reduces pressure on natural systems.
- **Intergenerational equity and legacy**: Regenerative thinking foregrounds the long-term impacts of today's actions, invoking moral responsibility to leave ecosystems in better condition for those who follow.

Media, education, art, and storytelling all play critical roles in circulating these narratives. Documentaries, exhibitions, literature, and community projects can bring regenerative ideas to life and make them relatable. Cultural institutions can act as conveners of dialogue and experimentation, creating spaces where new visions of the bioeconomy are imagined and enacted.

Public policy and corporate communications also contribute to shaping these narratives. Language choices—such as referring to waste as a resource, or framing food systems as cycles rather than supply chains—can shift perception and behavior. Participation in storytelling, particularly by communities affected by environmental degradation or already practicing regenerative methods, ensures inclusivity and legitimacy.

Ultimately, cultural narratives provide the emotional and symbolic foundation for large-scale change. They help build societal support for transformative policies, business models, and personal practices. Aligning bio-based transitions with narratives of regeneration enables a shift not only in systems and structures but in collective purpose and identity—toward an economy that restores, reconnects, and respects life.

Education, Communication, and Capacity-Building for Circular Mindsets

Transitioning to a nature-positive circular bioeconomy requires more than technical solutions—it demands a deep cultural and behavioral shift. Education, communication, and capacity-building are essential to fostering the circular mindsets needed across society to support regenerative systems, close resource loops, and prioritize ecological resilience. These efforts equip individuals, institutions, and communities with the knowledge, skills, and motivation to participate meaningfully in the transition.

Education at all levels—formal, informal, and lifelong learning—lays the foundation for circular thinking. In schools and universities, curricula can be updated to include systems thinking, life cycle analysis, biomaterials, ecological economics, and regenerative design. Interdisciplinary approaches help students understand the interconnectedness of environmental, economic, and social systems. Project-based learning and community engagement allow learners to apply circular principles in real-world contexts.

Technical and vocational education plays a key role in building skills for emerging circular bioeconomy jobs. This includes training in composting, biogas systems, organic waste collection, bio-based manufacturing, and sustainable farming practices. Upskilling existing workers helps ensure a just transition, particularly in regions dependent on linear or extractive industries.

Communication strategies raise awareness, influence public behavior, and create demand for circular products and services. Clear, relatable messaging helps explain circular concepts—such as regeneration, reuse, or biological cycles—in ways that connect with daily life. Visual storytelling, social media campaigns, and community events can illustrate the benefits of circular practices, counter misinformation, and build a shared sense of purpose.

Effective communication also involves transparency about product claims, environmental impacts, and supply chain practices. Labelling, certification, and digital product passports can inform consumers and increase trust in circular solutions. Engaging influencers, educators, and local leaders as advocates can amplify messaging and build social momentum.

Capacity-building involves strengthening the institutional, technical, and organizational ability of stakeholders to plan, implement, and scale circular bioeconomy initiatives. This includes:

- Supporting local governments in designing policies and procurement strategies that promote bio-based and regenerative products

- Helping small and medium-sized enterprises adopt circular business models and access relevant technologies
- Training community groups, cooperatives, and informal workers in organic waste management, local composting, or circular entrepreneurship
- Providing tools and guidance for educators, planners, and development agencies to integrate circular principles into their work

Participatory learning approaches—such as peer exchanges, living labs, and co-design workshops—help embed circular thinking in practice and foster innovation. These methods encourage collaboration across disciplines, sectors, and generations, supporting a whole-systems perspective.

Ultimately, shifting to a circular mindset means moving from extractive habits to regenerative responsibility, from linear consumption to cyclical value creation. Education, communication, and capacity-building are not just support mechanisms—they are central to shaping the values, knowledge, and skills that underpin a just and lasting circular bioeconomy.

Shaping Demand Through Public Procurement and Consumer Awareness

Stimulating demand for circular and bio-based products is critical to accelerating the transition to a nature-positive circular bioeconomy. Public procurement and consumer awareness are two powerful levers that influence markets, drive innovation, and normalize sustainable choices. Together, they help build the demand-side conditions needed to scale regenerative systems and shift economic activity away from extractive models.

Public procurement represents a significant share of national and local spending, particularly in sectors such as food services, construction, infrastructure, and packaging. By integrating circular and bioeconomy criteria into purchasing policies, governments can catalyze market demand for products that are renewable, recyclable, compostable, or made from recovered materials. This includes:

- Prioritizing bio-based materials in packaging, office supplies, uniforms, or building components
- Requiring compostable food packaging and organic waste separation in public catering services
- Specifying circular performance criteria—such as durability, repairability, or recyclability—in product tenders
- Sourcing locally produced compost, soil enhancers, or biomaterials to support regional bioeconomy loops

Public authorities can also use procurement as a demonstration tool, showcasing circular innovation and creating visibility for sustainable alternatives. Framework agreements, pre-commercial procurement, and supplier development programs can support small and medium-sized enterprises in entering public markets and scaling circular solutions.

Consumer awareness complements procurement by shaping preferences, habits, and purchasing decisions. Informed consumers are more likely to choose products that align with circular principles—such as reusable goods, products with minimal or compostable packaging, or items made from recycled or bio-based materials. Awareness efforts can include:

- Educational campaigns that explain the benefits of circularity and bio-based products in terms of climate, health, and ecosystem impact
- Clear labelling systems and digital product information that help consumers identify sustainable choices
- Marketing and storytelling that build emotional connections to regenerative lifestyles and emphasize quality, longevity, and purpose over quantity and disposability
- Retail partnerships that promote refill stations, return schemes, or eco-designed product lines

Behavior change tools such as nudges, social norms, or price incentives can further support consumers in adopting circular practices. For example, discounts for using reusable containers, loyalty programs for circular product use, or visible repair and reuse stations in public places can normalize more sustainable behavior.

To be effective, both procurement and awareness initiatives must be grounded in credible standards and supported by transparent monitoring. They should avoid greenwashing and ensure that claims about circularity, compostability, or bio-based content are verifiable and backed by lifecycle data.

Equity considerations are also important. Public campaigns and procurement programs should be inclusive, ensuring that all communities can access and benefit from circular products and services. This may involve subsidizing reusable alternatives, supporting community-led awareness efforts, or prioritizing small producers in procurement systems.

By aligning public procurement strategies with consumer engagement, governments and organizations can shape demand ecosystems that support the scale-up of circular bioeconomy solutions. This dual approach strengthens the pull for innovation, reinforces market signals, and accelerates the cultural and economic shift toward regenerative and nature-positive systems.

Inclusion and Equity in Circular Bioeconomy Transformations

Ensuring inclusion and equity in circular bioeconomy transformations is essential for achieving a just, sustainable, and socially resilient transition. While the circular bioeconomy offers opportunities for economic development, environmental regeneration, and innovation, these benefits are not automatically distributed evenly across populations. Without deliberate effort, transitions can exacerbate existing inequalities related to income, geography, gender, ethnicity, and access to resources or decision-making processes.

Equity in the circular bioeconomy means that all groups—especially those historically marginalized—have meaningful opportunities to participate in, shape, and benefit from new systems of production, consumption, and resource management. It also means addressing structural barriers that prevent participation and ensuring that the transition does not result in unintended social or ecological harms.

Key areas where inclusion and equity must be addressed include:

Access to land, biomass, and resources

Rural and Indigenous communities often steward landscapes rich in biomass and biodiversity, yet they may lack secure land tenure or face competition from large-scale bioeconomy enterprises. Policies should protect community rights, support equitable benefit-sharing from biomass use, and recognize traditional knowledge in resource management and innovation.

Participation in decision-making

Inclusive governance processes ensure that the voices of women, youth, Indigenous peoples, informal workers, and other underrepresented groups are considered in the design of circular bioeconomy policies, projects, and investments. Participatory planning, community consultations, and co-creation platforms can strengthen legitimacy, social buy-in, and cultural relevance.

Fair employment and decent work

Bioeconomy sectors can generate new jobs in regenerative agriculture, organic waste management, biomanufacturing, and ecological restoration. However, it is important to ensure that these jobs are accessible, fairly paid, safe, and offer social protection.

Skills development and training programs should reach diverse populations, including those in the informal sector, low-income areas, or transitioning out of declining industries.

Support for small-scale and community enterprises

Smallholders, cooperatives, and social enterprises are key actors in many circular bioeconomy value chains. Access to finance, infrastructure, markets, and capacity-building can help these actors scale up while maintaining local ownership and reinvestment in communities. Public procurement and certification systems can be designed to favor inclusive and socially responsible suppliers.

Gender equity

Women are often underrepresented in bioeconomy leadership and decision-making roles but play essential roles in agriculture, food systems, and informal recycling sectors. Circular bioeconomy initiatives should include gender-responsive design, promote women's leadership, and address barriers such as land access, credit, or time burdens.

Equitable access to circular products and services

Households with lower incomes may face challenges in affording circular alternatives such as reusable products, composting services, or bio-based materials. Policies can support affordability and access through subsidies, social pricing, and investment in inclusive circular infrastructure.

Recognition of informal and traditional systems

In many contexts, circular practices such as repair, reuse, organic farming, and community composting already exist outside formal markets. Recognizing and integrating these practices into formal bioeconomy planning can strengthen resilience, reduce duplication, and uphold cultural values.

Embedding inclusion and equity in circular bioeconomy transformations requires cross-sector collaboration, transparent metrics, and accountability mechanisms. Monitoring tools should track social outcomes—such as job quality, gender participation, and income distribution—alongside environmental and economic indicators.

By centering justice, participation, and fairness, the circular bioeconomy can become not only a tool for ecological regeneration but a pathway to more inclusive, resilient, and equitable societies.

Conclusion

The transition to a nature-positive circular bioeconomy offers a systemic pathway to regenerate ecosystems, reduce environmental pressures, and create resilient, inclusive economies. Unlike traditional linear models, circular bioeconomy systems prioritize renewable biological resources, closed-loop material cycles, and the restoration of nature as central principles. This transformation extends beyond technological innovation—it demands cultural change, institutional coordination, and equity-centered design.

Across sectors and scales, opportunities exist to reshape production, consumption, and governance through regenerative practices, material circularity, and socially inclusive approaches. From local composting systems and citizen science to industrial symbiosis and science-based targets, circular bioeconomy frameworks must operate within planetary boundaries while delivering tangible social and ecological benefits.

Achieving this vision requires aligning policy, investment, education, and public behavior around shared goals. It also requires new narratives and participatory processes that value biodiversity, community stewardship, and intergenerational responsibility. As cities, regions, and nations implement circular bioeconomy strategies, the focus must remain on creating systems that give back more to nature and society than they take.

The circular bioeconomy is not merely a technical fix but a holistic shift in how humanity interacts with the natural world—rooted in regeneration, collaboration, and long-term resilience.

www.ingramcontent.com/pod-product-compliance
Lightning Source LLC
Chambersburg PA
CBHW052138270326
41930CB00012B/2940